Insider's Guide to Quilting Careers

By
Merry May and Linda J. Hahn

First Printing, February 2009.

Published by QuiltWoman.com
16731 Powerline Rd. Holley, NY 14470
Toll Free 877-454-7967
info@quiltwoman.com

Printed in the United States of America

Publisher's Cataloging-in-Publication
(Provided by Quality Books, Inc.)

    May, Merry.
       Insider's guide to quilting careers / by Merry May
    and Linda Hahn.
       p. cm.
       Includes index.
       ISBN-13: 97809714501-2-7
       ISBN-10: 09714501-2-9

       1. Quilting--Vocational guidance.   I. Hahn, Linda.
    II. Title.

    TT835.M27369 2009   746.46'023
                       QBI09-200022

ISBN 0-9714501-2-9

DEDICATION

We dedicate this book to our husbands, Allan Hahn and Joe May.

We thank you from the bottom of our hearts for the love, understanding and support you give us. Although our quilting adventures may take us away from home from time to time, know that you are always in our thoughts and hearts.

Love,

Linda and Merry

Acknowledgements

We wish to thank Nancy Dill and the team at QuiltWoman.com for "taking us on".

We also wish to thank all the quilt professionals - Dana Balsamo, Kris Dreissen, Madge Ziegler, Michele Scott, B.J. Titus, Jean Ann Wright, Carrie Nelson, Lacey June Hill, John Scibran, Cher Hurney, Rita B. Barber, Pat Moore, Lorraine Fenstermacher, Cyndi Souder, Gail Kessler, Lisa Shepard Stewart, Elizabeth Shnayder, Vikki Pignatelli, Mindy Casperson, Deloa Jones, Carol Newman, Geri Wolf and Rebecca Szabo - who so generously shared their knowledge and experience for our research.

Additionally, we thank our other professionals, Lyle Sandler, Kevin Meszaros, CPA, Christina Manuella, Esq. and Chuck Casagrande for contributing sub-chapters on their specific specialty. Thank you to Morna McEver Golletz for writing our Forward.

We also want to give a big thank you and a hug to our proofreaders, Robin L. Sandler and Jane M. Hand.

And of course, to our families for putting up with us and supporting us in all of our endeavors.

Linda and Merry

Foreword

Welcome to a fabulous industry! I've been involved with quilting since the 1970s and began to earn money from my quilting a few years later. As you'll discover in the Insider's Guide to Quilting Careers, you can make your career in quilting what you want – large, small, full-time, part-time. After discovering my passion in quilting, I've been a teacher, a designer, a commission quilter, a writer and the owner of a fine-arts cooperative, and I've sold finished quilts on consignment and at fine craft shows. Today I publish The Professional Quilter, a business quarterly for professionals, and teach business classes to quilters and other fiber artists.

My career has seen me through several decades and multiple cross-state family moves. It's also introduced me to many fascinating people, and I've made lifelong friends. Two of the people I've met along the way are Linda Hahn and Merry May. Both have found success as teachers, and they'll introduce you to a vast world of opportunities.

One thing all professionals agree on is that you wear lots of hats in this business. Linda's worn hats as teacher and, most recently, as longarm quilter. Merry's primary hat is also as teacher, though she's done a long stint as a pattern designer, particularly of mysteries. While most of us in the industry wear more than one hat, Merry and Linda also sought out the experts who were wearing hats they weren't. You'll learn from shop owners and show organizers, competition quilters and fabric designers. And you'll learn about how networking with other professionals can help your career.

Something all professionals also agree on is that your career is going to change. You may start as a teacher and then decide to market your patterns. Or you may be a teacher and find your place as a longarm quilter. Or you may decide after vending at smaller shows to open a quilt shop. When I started many of my ventures, it was largely trial and error. You'll have a handy reference in the Insider's Guide to Quilting Careers to get you started. And, you'll find the Resources chapter a valuable source for more information.

As I stated at the beginning of this forward, welcome to a fabulous industry. Jump aboard, but most of all, and enjoy the journey!

Morna McEver Golletz
Publisher/Editor
The Professional Quilter
www.professionalquilter.com

Table of Contents

Introduction

Just about every quilter dreams at some time or another of quitting his or her day job and working in some aspect of the quilting industry.

With this book, we hope to introduce you to the numerous career opportunities which are available within the quilt world, as well as provide you with information on how to get started, get noticed, how much money you need to invest, income potential, job descriptions and more.

We do not claim to be experts in every area. During our writing process, we sought out and interviewed people who do, in fact, work in each area on a regular basis. We are forever indebted to them for candidly sharing their vast knowledge with us. We are quilters first and foremost - quilt professionals second. As quilt professionals, we should be sharing and teaching not only the art of quilting but also mentoring and guiding the development of the quilt professionals of the future.

The book is written for both the professional and non-professional quilter. You may be a quilter who is merely curious about the various careers, you could be the quilter who is beginning their career as a quilt professional (in any area) or you may be a professional quilter seeking information on other avenues of income.

After our research was done and the chapters drafted, we forwarded them to two ladies with different levels of experience - Jane M. Hand and Robin L. Sandler. These ladies carefully reviewed each chapter and provided input about material that needed a little more explanation and additional questions they had. In this way, we tried to ensure that we provided as much in-depth information as possible. We thank them from the bottoms of our hearts for volunteering to do this for us!

We hope you will use this book as a reference guide for your future endeavors.

Linda J. Hahn and Merry D. May
Double Trouble Studios

Chapter One
General Information

How do I know I am ready to move into the professional level? For the most part, no one really seems to have started out with a goal of becoming a quilt professional – it just seems to happen. However, those who are successful have also invested a lot of hard work and in most cases, talent and ambition. There are a handful of quilters who develop a new technique or pattern, shoot to "stardom" and become an "in demand" teacher instantly. In most cases, though, it can take ten or more years to become an "overnight success."

What exactly IS a quilt professional? You are a professional if you:

- Make baby quilts to sell to people you work with
- Teach in exchange for pay
- Quilt and/or finish another person's project for pay
- Win several first-place awards in judged quilt shows
- Make quilts to sell at craft shows, through consignment, online, and/or in galleries
- Make custom quilts for others (for example, memory quilts or t-shirt quilts)
- Design quilts and sell your own patterns
- Sell your designs to magazines
- Own a quilt shop
- Do appraisals for others
- Repair other people's quilts
- Vend at a quilt show
- Judge quilts at a quilt show or county or state fair

In addition, there are other careers such as fabric designing, being a fabric salesperson, writing books, being a magazine editor, organizing quilting retreats, or managing a large quilt show for profit. You could also work for a company that manufactures fabric, or is a distributor of fabrics and notions, or even at a quilt shop.

Obviously some of these jobs have regular business hours, while others do not. Some require a trip to an office, while others can work at home. The best part is that you get to decide what kind of work you wish to do, and choose one or more activities that fit into your individual lifestyle.

Many of us will combine several careers and work full-time to earn some extra money. This requires a bit of organization in order to fulfill the demands of a diverse group of jobs. There are those who thrive on this, and there are those who struggle with juggling many different commitments.

This is the case with Merry and Linda; they each have a number of "irons in the fire" at any given time. Collectively, they manage to bring in a fairly steady income, which at the very least is enough to feed their fabric "needs" and in Linda's case, pay for her family to go on cruises on a regular basis.

Depending upon the line – or lines – of work you wish to pursue, you may need to develop a resumé, a portfolio, or a web site. All of these enable potential clients to take a look at your accomplishments so far, and decide whether or not they will "hire" you to provide one or more of your services.

RESUMÉ

If you are ever asked to participate as an exhibitor in a gallery show, or to present a workshop or lecture for a guild, show or retreat, you may be asked to provide a copy of your resumé.

In most cases, a one-page resumé will be sufficient; more than one page tends to be a bit overdone and superfluous. We have included a sample resumé in our Forms section.

To get started building your resumé, you need to organize your work experience into different categories. Some categories could include:

- Education, both formal (college) and quilt related.

- Quilt-Related Work Experience: Begin with a very brief description of how and when you began your quilting career (one sentence), and continue to add to the list as you gain more experience. When you are starting out, you can include such things as presenting a lecture for your local guild, teaching at local Adult Education programs, or teaching at a local quilt shop.

- Quilt-Related Memberships and Activities: Should include local, regional, national and international groups to whom you pay dues. You may also include any Board or Committee positions you may have chaired or been active in.

- Awards and Recognitions: If you won a Viewer's Choice award, or any awards from a judged show, during your local guild's show, list it here.

- Publications: Have you sent photos in to a magazine and had them printed in one of the issues? Did you write an article for a magazine or newspaper and have it published?
- Exhibits: This is for things like gallery exhibits, including being part of a group exhibit. Was one of your quilts accepted into a traveling exhibit? List it here!
- Other Hobbies and Interests: Try to include one or two things that most people would not know about you. Sometimes if you can make the reader laugh, you can get the job!

As you gain more experience, start to weed out the less important events in order to draw more attention to the more important ones. Eventually you may run out of space on your one-page resumé and need to reduce the size of your type (font) in order to squeeze all of the important things in.

See our sample Resumé in our Forms section.

WHAT IS A PORTFOLIO, AND WHY DO I NEED ONE?

If you are in any of the categories of making quilts for others, teaching, doing longarm quilting, restoration work, or designing, a portfolio is a very handy thing to have. Some people make their portfolios in the traditional way, with paper and an actual book. Others use web sites and/or Blogs to promote themselves and their work.

A portfolio is basically a way for you to showcase your accomplishments and abilities while promoting yourself.

One important thing to remember is that a portfolio is not a scrapbook! You want your portfolio to look inviting and attractive, while providing the viewer with a "visual resumé." In other words, keep it clean looking and concise. Update it every few months to keep it fresh. Be sure to include your written resumé, which should also be kept current.

When assembling your portfolio, ask yourself, "what am I promoting?" It is acceptable to divide your portfolio into several different categories, illustrating your strength in several areas. For example, Merry's portfolio is divided into the following "chapters:"

- Quiltmaker
- Designer
- Instructor
- Innovator

Merry then illustrates her abilities in each category with photos, news clippings, printed programs, sketches, and other items which illustrate her strengths in each area. She does not include work that she does not wish to perform on a regular basis, such as doing restoration work.

Other things to include in your portfolio are:

- Your resumé
- Your Artist's Statement or a brief Introduction summarizing your work
- Business cards
- Brochure for viewers to take with them; could include classes if you teach, or a price list if you do commission work or longarm quilting
- Brief captions with the photos if needed

You may also wish to make a few pieces specifically for your portfolio, just to show and/or challenge your abilities and explore new territory.

Document your work on a consistent basis. This includes taking a photo of every quilt you make immediately after completing it, and writing down some basic information about the quilt. At the very least, write the date you completed the quilt, the dimensions of the quilt, and perhaps a sentence about why you made it; if it is for sale, where you plan to sell it or to whom you plan to sell it. Even if you just jot this information onto a sticky note and attach it to the back of a photograph of the quilt, it will help you to remember this basic information and be able to accurately convey some of the details about the piece at a later date. Merry firmly believes in doing this, because, she says, "Two weeks from now, will you remember any of this information? I think not."

Ask yourself every now and then, "what have I done lately that belongs in my portfolio?" You will want to periodically update it, too. Merry uses clear page protectors in a leather notebook so it is easy to change the pages.

One other thing you want to consider is asking someone else to look over your portfolio before you present it to the public for the first time. Ask them to look for spelling and grammar errors, and ask them to be honest about whether the information is well organized so it makes sense.

When it is time to review and update your portfolio, the old adage, "If in doubt, throw it out" is a good mantra to repeat to yourself.

Although some people think physical portfolios are a thing of the past and rely on having a web site as their portfolio, Merry has encountered a number of occasions when it was quite helpful to have a portfolio. This included when she was recently doing an artist in residence appearance, and when she was the featured quilter at the New Jersey Quilt Convention. You can't always have your laptop for people to look at, but you can have a hands-on portfolio. To Merry the physical portfolio is much more personal than having photos on a computer.

That being said, there is also a valid argument for having an online portfolio as well. It enables many more people to be exposed to your work. You may also wish to have your photos on your iPod or mp3 player, in order to show your work on the spot. Although you won't have all of the details about each piece, at least you can offer a potential client a look at what you have done in the past.

ETHICAL CONCERNS

While each area of the quilt industry has its own specific ethical concerns, there are many which can apply to the entire industry. You as an individual must decide how you will handle each issue, depending upon how they deal with your particular business and your position in the quilt industry.

Copyright raises its ugly head constantly. Do not under any circumstances make copies of a book or pattern for someone. It is important that you, as a quilt professional, set an example. If you overhear someone in your class telling another student not to buy a pattern because they'll just copy theirs – use the opportunity to educate. Don't just say "no you can't do that" – educate them as to why it is not acceptable to do that.

Speaking poorly of another quilt professional is in very poor taste. There is no reason to "badmouth" another professional, no matter how true it may be. In a classroom situation, do not say, "Mary Bagodonuts doesn't know what she is doing – do it my way". Everyone has their own way of doing things, and there is always more than one way to do nearly every aspect of quiltmaking. Students may feel more comfortable with one teacher's style than another. You do not need to badmouth someone else in order to get ahead. There is plenty of room for all of us, because we each have a unique contribution to make. If Mary Bagodonuts isn't doing a good job, she will soon be out of work, even without your influence. At worst, she could hear about your criticism and confront you about it face to face.

NETWORKING and PLAYING NICELY WITH OTHERS

Networking with other quilt professionals is how we were able to secure a great deal of the information for this book. Networking is simply talking with other people who are in the same profession as yourself, and sharing information back and forth. Those who have more experience than you can provide you with valuable information on how they worked their way up the career ladder; those with less experience may have a few tips they are willing to share with you as well.

The Quilt Professionals' Network is a networking group in the Mid-Atlantic region. Members come from at least six different states, and work in numerous areas of the quilting industry, at all different levels. Once a year, "QPN" members meet for a three-day conference of continuing education. One important part of the weekend is having opportunities to network and get to know one another better. Even if some of us are working in the same area, we all have different experiences. Networking enables us to learn from each other, and hopefully avoid some of the pitfalls that are common in our particular area of expertise.

Sharing information is something that is important to both Merry and Linda. Merry tells a story about the first time she decided to be a vendor at Quilt Market. She and a couple of friends were visiting a local quilt shop before Market opened. She noticed two other ladies in the shop who were talking about being in the area for Quilt Market. Merry asked one of them a question pertaining to one of the events at Market that she was unfamiliar with. The response? "This is all trial by fire; figure it out for yourself."

This was an enlightening moment for Merry, and it was also when she decided that things did not need to be this difficult for others to learn the ropes. She dedicated her career to helping others learn the ins and outs of the quilting profession, which ultimately led to her collaboration with Linda to write this book.

PRINTED MATTERS

When it comes to presenting yourself in print, it really does matter how your brochures, flyers and business cards look.

For consistency's sake, we are primarily discussing brochure design, but the examples below apply to business cards and flyers as well.

Doing graphic design may not be your cup of tea, but the chances are good that you know someone else who is good at it, or at least has a flair for it. This is one of those times when networking can pay off. When you see someone's brochure that is attractive and well laid out, ask them who did their brochure design. If it is them, you are well on your way to negotiating a deal of some kind, where this person provides a nice brochure for you, and you do something that you specialize in for them. If it was someone else who designed the brochure, perhaps you can hire the same person to design a brochure, flyer and/or business card for you.

To find some help online, use your favorite search engine to bring up "free brochure design." You will have many choices, but be careful before making a commitment to order "free" samples. Some sites will charge you to upload your file, and will also charge high rates for shipping and handling. Some of the sites provide free templates where you may copy and paste your information into the appropriate places in the templates. Be sure to inquire if any purchase you make will allow you to print your own copies once the initial sale is completed.

Once you have an original printout of the brochure, you then need to copy it in small quantities so you can begin to distribute it. We highly recommend that you start off with small quantities, because you will want to update the information somewhat frequently, especially when you are just getting started.

You may also wish to consider hiring someone to design a logo for you. Sometimes you can work through a local community college by calling their graphic design department. Ask if any of the students might be willing to design a logo for you – and quite possibly a brochure and business cards as well.

Whatever you decide to do, make sure you end up with promotional items that are attractive and easy to read. Ask others to take a look at the proof copy and give you some feedback. They may notice spelling and grammar errors that you didn't see before, or they might find that you forgot to include the rates you charge for your lectures and workshops.

The bottom line is, if you don't take your promotional items seriously, no one else is obligated to do so.

Chapter Two
Shop Owner

QUILT SHOP OWNERSHIP

The most visible and most dreamed about career in the quilt industry (according to our survey) is quilt shop ownership. Many people think they will be able to sew all day, while customers come in and buy their beautiful fabric. There is much more to shop ownership than this. When you open the door to your shop, it is first and foremost a business. You have a lot invested in it, and a lot to lose if you fail. On the other hand, there are many successful shop owners whose primary income is generated by their shop.

GETTING STARTED

One of the first things you need to address is a business plan. In the sidebar you will find a sample of the possible expenses involved in starting up a quilt shop. As you can see, you will need almost $100,000 to prepare to open your doors. We have included several web sites with

Security Deposit (1 1/2 x monthly rent)	$2250
First Month's Rent	$1500
Legal & Professional Fees	$250
Inspection Fees	$300
Signs	$2500
Utility Deposits	$500
Fixtures	$7000
Paint & Carpeting	$3500
Inventory @ $50 per square foot (1200 s.f.)	$60,000
Advertising	$1000
Payroll & Annual Party	$1000
Office Equipment	$5000
Insurance	$2500
Approximate Total:	$87, 300

business plan templates in our Resource section for you to explore.

You need to search for a location in your chosen geographical area. Perhaps you may choose an older home, a strip mall location off a busy road, or even a quaint shop located along a main street. You may choose to purchase the building or lease the location.

In choosing your location, you need to take numerous things into consideration such as parking, outside lighting, ingress and egress into the shop (especially for your handicapped or older customers), and your competition. Are there places to eat within walking distance to your shop?

If you lease space, you may be subject to contribute to a common area maintenance fee, and perhaps the real estate taxes. Rent is usually based on square footage for a fixed length of time. A security deposit is usually required. You may also opt for a "stand alone" space, such as a converted house. This rent may include all costs in one fixed price - this price may or may not include utilities. You obviously need to consult with an attorney to review the lease.

You need to check with the municipality where your shop will be located to ascertain whether you need any permits, fire inspections or a certificate of occupancy. If you are going to put up a sign, you also need to check if there are any specific requirements as to permits, size or type.

Signage may take some time, and it is advantageous to hire someone from the area, in that they would be most familiar with the municipal requirements.

Rebecca Szabo of Creative Sew n Sews feels that THE most important part of opening a shop is to be REALISTIC.

You must be a business owner first. Just because you love to quilt does not mean you can open up the shop and quilt all day. You must work really hard for little financial reward. Most days you will be too busy being a shop owner to be a quilter!

If you have not already done so, you need to establish a relationship with a reputable accountant who will guide you through the maze of balancing your books, paying sales tax, insurance, payroll taxes and reporting your income properly.

Establish a Return Policy, and be sure to post it prominently. Also be aware of laws concerning time limits on gift certificates.

FURNISHINGS AND DISPLAYS

The interior of your new shop might need some painting, carpeting or other improvements. You may want to utilize the services of family members (kids might work for pizza)! If you are lucky, your spouse might be handy with the hammer and can customize some fixtures and furniture for you.

Search your local home improvement stores, a used furniture store or perhaps an office supply store. You need safe, comfortable chairs for your classroom.

Once your store is prepared and furnished, it's time to stock the shelves! The shop owners who participated in our interviews indicated that inventory should be a minimum of $50 per square foot of the store. Your inventory needs to include fabric, notions, patterns, books and thread.

INVENTORY

We are assuming that you already have your business license and have consulted tax and insurance professionals for your appropriate forms and filings.

You will need to open an account with a distributor, such as Checker Distributors, United Notions or Brewer Sewing Supplies (see our Resource section for more information). Depending on your credit history, you may be able to choose to have the merchandise billed on a credit card or on a 30 day net basis. You will find that each distributor will carry different merchandise, so it is a good idea to open accounts with more than one distributor. You may find that you prefer one distributor (for whatever reason - having more of the supplies you want in stock, promptness in shipping) than the other. You can also order directly from the designer, but they may have a minimum order.

It is very important that you stock your store with a variety of fabrics, notions and patterns that appeal to many types of quilters, rather than purchasing only what appeals to you. Not everyone likes batiks, for example.

Budget your funds - you need to maintain a balanced inventory - once established you will see what the trends of the shoppers are in your area.

OFFICE & MISCELLANEOUS EQUIPMENT

You will need a cash register, calculator, telephone system, computer, copier, fax machine and a credit card processing machine. Please refer to our chapter on Business Issues for more in-depth information about credit card processing.

ADVERTISEMENT

If you do not yet have an established customer base, you might be able to purchase a mailing list from a store that is closing.

Otherwise some other ways to build a customer base are:

- Send out announcements to local quilt guilds
- Put out flyers at grocery store bulletin boards, local guild meetings and shows, perhaps with a coupon which will enable you to track where the customer picked up their flyer.
- Sponsor a judged category at a quilt show
- List your shop on the numerous free web listings (see Resources)
- Establish your own web site and encourage people to sign up for weekly e-mail updates (see Business Issues for more about web sites).

Some guilds have a policy that their membership list is not to be used for commercial purposes, so be cautious where any mailing list comes from.

Establishing a newsletter on a regular basis is very important once you have gathered names and addresses and/or e-mails. This will keep your customers informed about classes, hours, special sales, and events.

A few "no-no"s:

- It is very inappropriate to place your shop's flyers in another quilt shop!
- Giving out incorrect directions to other quilt shops is just not nice, and it will also come back to haunt you!
- Never, never, never photocopy books

or patterns thinking that it will lower your expenses. In the long run it can cause you to close your shop when you are sued by the copyright owners whose livelihoods you have affected.

TEACHERS

We will address the issue of teaching at a quilt shop in our "Teaching" chapter from the teacher's point of view. In this chapter, we will address teaching from the shop owner's point of view.

All of our interviewed shop owners indicated that they find their teachers by reaching out to talented quilters in their areas.

One New Jersey quilt shop pays the teachers a set hourly rate of $15 per hour for 1-3 students in a class, and increases that to $25 per hour for four or more. Payment in this way allows the shop to run the class with low enrollment. The shop may choose to run a class with low enrollment if the students are special customers of the shop.

Another shop allows the teachers to decide how much to charge per student, and then adds a 25% surcharge onto that. For example, if a teacher sets a fee of $20 per student, the shop charges the student $25. The surcharge covers some of the shop's expenses for electricity, newsletter mailings, and overhead.

Most shops must limit the number of students in their classes because of space limitations.

Teachers in our interviewed shops receive anywhere from a 10% to a 50% discount during the time that they are on the shop's teaching schedule.

Shop owners request that the teacher submit a clean, current class sample (preferably using fabric from their shop) along with a supply list and class description before the newsletter is published. Early or on-time submissions enable the shop to secure the required supplies for their students. There is nothing more frustrating than going to a class and finding that the shop was unable to obtain the required supplies in time for the class. Teachers are sometimes permitted to bring in specialty items that are not carried by the store. In this case, the shop may negotiate or ask for a percentage of the sales.

Students usually receive a modest discount on the supplies purchased for the class.

It is usually in the financial interest of the teacher to teach at only one local shop per quarter, or at least to not teach the same class at more than one location within the same period of time.

PARTICIPATING IN A REGIONAL SHOP HOP

Every shop hop will have its own set of guidelines established by those who are participating in it. There may be as few as five shops, or as many as ten or more involved. It usually takes at least a year to plan all of the details of the shop hop, which means mandatory meetings among the shop owners at least on a quarterly basis. Most also keep in touch by e-mail between meetings.

Some of the decisions to be made include:

• Monetary contributions from each shop to cover expenses such as the prizes, giveaways, advertising and such.

- Hours for the shops to be open; all shops should keep the same hours during the shop hop.
- Agreements on not having special sales during the shop hop, other than the shop's usual sale section.
- Price for Passports, which include directions to each shop, space for stamping as hoppers travel from shop to shop, hours, and the rules.
- Agree on a date for the shop hop; depending on the number of shops involved and their proximity, this can vary from three consecutive days to several weekends.
- Decide on the values of the main prizes, and what the rules are for hoppers to qualify to win the main prizes.
- Choose one or more quilt designs for hoppers to collect as they travel from shop to shop; divide up the work needed to make a sample.
- Make arrangements for the shop hop quilt to travel from shop to shop, if necessary; or, each shop makes their own sample to display.
- Designating different shop owners to be responsible for various aspects of the hop; for example, who will manage the group's funds for the prizes and such?

Participation in a shop hop can be beneficial by building a broader customer base and enabling shop owners to network with one another.

It is important that all shops share in the work required for a successful shop hop.

Most groups have a meeting immediately after the shop hop ends to distribute prizes, and to analyze the results of the shop hop.

QUILT MARKET

As we will mention throughout this book, you should make every effort to attend Quilt Market as often as possible, but especially when it is in your region.

Quilt Market is a huge semiannual wholesale show. It is held in Houston, Texas in the fall, and in various locations in the spring. This is the place for all of the latest patterns, books, fabrics, notions, and many other things you never knew you needed! You will meet famous quilters, see the latest trends, and be exhausted by the end of each day. Be sure to wear your most comfortable walking shoes because you will need them!

Quilt Market is only open to those who are involved in the quilting industry. You are required to submit your business credentials for approval prior to registering.

There is a full day of classes called "Schoolhouse" where vendors provide detailed information about new products or techniques. There are seminars, workshops, and of course the all-important lunch break, which allows shop owners valuable time to network while resting their tired feet.

Some of the bigger vendors will have elaborate parties either before Market opens, or on one of the evenings after hours.

Another event to consider is "Sample Spree" where shop owners can purchase pre-made samples or get special deals from the vendors the evening before Quilt Market opens. Be prepared for crowds and chaos at Sample Spree, because everyone is scrambling to make their way to the "best" vendors for the best deals.

PROMOTIONS

Promotions are a great traffic booster! You can send postcards or e-mails one week ahead several times a year, such as for Christmas in July, Sew Thankful Day in November, Anniversary Sale, or Inventory Reduction Sale at the end of the year. You could also offer gift idea demo days, sponsor a QuiltPink Day, host a monthly gathering for Project Linus, for example.

Be aware that sometimes sending out sale notifications can cause a drop in your business shortly before the sale date. Some customers will come in advance to choose what they wish to purchase during the sale, and some will also ask you to extend the sale terms to them before the sale. Be very careful about bending the rules, because word will spread like wildfire.

VENDING

Vending is a great way to increase awareness of your shop. Most of our interviewees vend only at area shows to increase visibility of their shop, and often to distribute coupons or flyers encouraging show attendees to visit their shop during or after the show.

Your booth should look clean, organized and professional. Include a variety of merchandise from your shop, especially items which other vendors may not carry, or which make your shop unique.

Make a list of items you must take with you (such as a cash register and credit card processing equipment), so you won't forget anything important.

Some shows provide tables, others rent them, and still others do not provide any tables at all. Be sure you know about the tables before you arrive!

Please see our chapter about Vending for much more information.

WORKING WITH AREA LONG ARM QUILTERS

Some shops prefer to work with one long arm quilter while others hand out business cards for all of the area long arm quilters, enabling the customer to choose among them.

As a courtesy, many shops will permit long arm quilters to drop off and pick up clients' quilts at their shop. This arrangement can be beneficial to the shop because it generates additional foot traffic and the potential for increased sales. Some shops ask for a cut of the long arm quilter's fee; others simply ask for a discount when the long arm quilter is doing work on shop samples.

Please see our chapter on Long Arm Quilting for much more information on this topic.

Other Resources -
American Quilt Retailer Magazine

Chapter Three
Teacher

TEACHING

Other than owning your own quilt shop, one of the most common and visible careers in the quilt industry is that of the quilt teacher. In this chapter, we will sub-divide teaching into several different levels. Not everyone is cut out to be a quilt teacher, but there are some who are better at teaching at one level than another. There are several levels of teaching, and sometimes one can lead into another.

Many people look at quilt teachers who travel from guild to guild and think these people are overpaid. What the general public does not know, however, is the amount of work that went into becoming a traveling teacher, how grueling it can be to travel from place to place, and how much time it takes to get from Point A to Point B. Chances are that years of hard work went into becoming an "overnight success."

Most people who teach quilting did not intend to go into this field of work. In many cases, people they know (such as fellow quilt guild members) saw their work and encouraged them to teach a group of people how to do the techniques or projects they are being shown. You may show a quilt at your guild's show and tell and be asked to teach a class on it. You may know how to quilt and your church group asks you to teach a group. At first you are flattered that someone wants to learn something from you, but then reality sets in: how do I do this? What should I include on my supply list? How do I describe the class to others? How much should I charge? What if I forget something important? What if I make a mistake? What if I'm too nervous? Do I need to be certified as a teacher?

You must be patient and able to effectively communicate instructions in several ways to students who may be at different skill levels. Not everyone learns in the same manner, and some students have learning disabilities. Teaching at your local adult education class is very different from teaching at a national level quilt show.

The more you teach, the more you will develop your own style. You need to understand that not every student will be able to work with your particular style. There are some teachers who are very rigid and insist on complete accuracy, while there are others who are on the more casual side. Every time you take a class with a teacher, take notice of how they pack their "stuff", how they present their material, how they deal with difficult or needy students, and how they present their supply lists and instructions. Think about the classes you have enjoyed and why you enjoyed (or didn't enjoy) them. Listen to your friends' reviews of the class with objectivity.

Once you decide to take the plunge into teaching, you will have a lot of questions. We hope to help you in making your way through the maze that can lead you to success.

TEACHING WORKSHOPS: GET YOURSELF ORGANIZED

The first things the students need for a workshop are:
- An accurate description of the class, including the finished size of the project. Most people appreciate seeing a photograph of the project as well
- How much is the fee for them to take the class?
- How many hours is the class, and should they bring their lunch?
- Will they be able to complete the project in class?
- What supplies will they need?
- What level of experience do they need in order to be successful in this class?
- Where will the class be held?
- Is it easy to get in and out of the classroom?
- Do they need extra money for any special supplies they must purchase from you?

The first issue, therefore, is accurately communicating the answers to the above questions as clearly and concisely as possible. But before you can do that, you have some other decisions to make.

How much time will the students need to complete, or at least understand, the project you are presenting to them? Most experienced teachers double the amount of time it takes them to complete a task in order to estimate the amount of class time needed. So if it takes you an hour to make a quilt block, figure on it taking the class about two hours. With this in mind, how much can you teach in a one-day (usually 6 or 7 hours) class? Is it possible for you to convey the same amount of information in a half-day class (usually about 3 hours)? Can you accomplish more if you have the students do some prep work (example, cutting their fabrics, and/or sometimes making certain basic units like half-square triangles) before they come to class? Obviously any prep work will need to be described in detail in the supply list you prepare.

THE SUPPLY LIST

Your supply list should be clear and concise. A photo is always helpful of the class project. DO NOT assume that everyone knows that they need to bring scissors and thread (even though they are quilting basics). At some point in time, you will have a student who does not bring something as basic as thread and will say that "it wasn't on the supply list".

Supply lists should, at a minimum, include:

- Your name
- Your contact information (phone, address, e-mail)
- The copyright symbol and the year in which you prepare your supply list – for example, ©2008 Merry May; Merry also includes the words, "All Rights Reserved" on any paperwork she hands out. (We will cover copyrights in another chapter.)
- Name of the class
- Brief description of the class
- List of supplies needed, broken down into categories such as "fabrics," and "other supplies" See our Forms section for some sample supply lists.

Besides making a lesson plan or notes about how the class should progress, it is suggested that you prepare step-by-step samples, especially for some of the more complex portions of your project. This way you can demonstrate the process much more efficiently without taking up a lot of valuable class time.

HANDOUTS

Some teachers are very generous with providing detailed handouts for their class, while some will provide handouts containing a limited amount of materials, the details of which must be obtained through class participation. Some teachers feel that if they give out extensive handouts, they are leaving themselves open to copyright violations. Other teachers will print their handouts with watermarks or on colored paper, or leave out essential details about a particular technique they intend to demonstrate in class. Be sure to read our chapter on Business Issues for much more about copyrights and related issues. While it is difficult to prevent, there ARE students out there who will take a class, and then teach that class to their friends or guild using photocopied class handouts. By doing this they are stealing potential income from you.

How you prepare your classroom handouts is a personal choice. Some basic information to include is: your name plus the copyright symbol and the year, the name of the class, and an outline of the steps necessary to complete the project or learn the technique. You may also include diagrams or photos of different steps, if you wish. Many students find illustrations to be very useful when they go to work on their projects at home after the class is over. It is also helpful to include your contact information in case they have questions at some point once they are at home. This could be in the form of your telephone number or e-mail. It gives the students a little boost of confidence that you are not going to "abandon" them once the formal class is over.

PRESENTING LECTURES AND PROGRAMS

When you feel you are ready to present a program, the best place to start is at your local guild. Speak with your guild's Program Chair to see when she might have an opening for a program. She will need to have some information on what you are planning to teach, such as the title of the program, and a paragraph or two about it to share with the guild through the monthly newsletter.

Planning a lecture usually begins when you have a topic you are very familiar with, and have a unique viewpoint to offer. Quilters love to see real quilts, so if you are demonstrating a technique, be sure to build up a good supply of samples. For one thing, making multiple samples will help you to focus on some of the intricacies of the technique you will be teaching. Sometimes you can even discover new shortcuts or clever ways to do the work as you are making your samples.

The first thing you need to do is write an outline, targeting the main points of your presentation. It is always a good idea to begin with some background on the topic, where you can educate your audience on how the technique originated, by whom (if known – be sure to give credit where credit is due), and perhaps why the technique came about.

Next is a step-by-step demonstration of the technique, which means having a series of partially completed projects to exhibit. It is best to make all of the samples with the same fabrics for consistency's sake, so your audience will be able to follow the progression.

The end of the presentation should tie up all the loose ends, and summarize everything you already covered. Be sure to ask if there are any questions. Sometimes your audience will point out things you never considered, or may lead you into learning more about your topic for your next presentation. Don't forget to thank the guild for inviting you to present your program to them.

Follow up with a nice thank you note to the Program Chair shortly after the presentation.

TRAVEL WARDROBE, ACCESSORIES, NECESSITIES

If you are teaching in a shop, the shop can provide you with guidelines on what is acceptable attire for that particular shop. Some shops do not allow open toe shoes (for safety reasons), others ask for a dress code that reflects the theme of the shop.

Common sense will tell you to look as professional as you can whenever or wherever you teach. There are times when you might be teaching at a retreat when jeans are acceptable, and there are other times when a nice business suit is appropriate. Even when jeans ARE acceptable, be sure to wear a nice blouse or sweater in order to dress the jeans up as much as you can. Merry's guideline is to wear something that, if an outsider walks into the room, they will be able to identify the teacher right away.

If you are traveling a long distance, you are more than likely limited to the size and weight of your suitcases and therefore need to make the most of what you can fit into one suitcase. First and foremost a pair of comfortable, flat shoes is in order. This is not the time to wear the "hot" shoes you just purchased that are for looks, and not for walking or standing. You will be on your feet for at least 6 hours at a workshop.

For clothing, we suggest travel knits because they shed wrinkles so well. There are companies now that sell individual coordinating pieces just for this purpose.

When you eventually begin to travel to teach, you may wish to have a travel bag filled and ready to pack and go, which contains everything you need – cleanser, moisturizer, toothpaste, etc. Many cosmetic companies offer free gifts with purchase opportunities. Take advantage of these offers.

Don't forget to include aspirin, Tums, antidiarrheal medicine, allergy meds, tweezers or even a gel mask. As odd as it may sound, having a spare set of underwear is also a good idea to always have on hand when traveling. You never know when you might miss a connecting flight and be stuck somewhere overnight without your luggage.

CALENDAR

Linda uses a loose-leaf notebook with monthly calendar pages printed and placed into page protectors. She also places a copy of any teaching contracts and copies of the hotel reservation for the event (vending, teaching, etc) in the sleeve for that month.

In addition to that, she maintains a separate folder (a tip learned from Merry) for each guild presentation that she is contracted for, and keeps them in chronological order. Each folder contains: copies of the supply list, contracts, directions and/or e-ticket information, printouts of all e-mail correspondence, notes from telephone conversations, shipping receipts, room set-up instructions, and anything else which may be pertinent to the trip.

You should make someone in your household aware of how you organize your engagements and where the paperwork can be found – just in case of an emergency if they need to cancel your engagements.

CERTIFICATION

At some point you may wish to become a certified quilting teacher. There are a couple of organizations which offer certification for teaching quilt making: the National Quilting Association and the Embroiderer's Guild of America.

Linda is a certified teacher through the NQA. This means that she has proven that she is qualified to teach Basic Quilting. To become certified, Linda had a Mentor who guided her through the certification process.

The certification process is similar to an independent study program. The candidate must make and submit a Honey Bee block along with answers to a Questionnaire. The candidate is then accepted or rejected. If accepted, the candidate proceeds through three stages of the certification process. The first is the submission of requested paperwork outlining the candidate's basic quilt making course. The second is the submission of samples of the candidate's work. Once the candidate is passed through the first two steps, he or she will present themselves at an evaluation panel. The evaluation panels are held at the annual show in Columbus, Ohio. More specifics on the Certified Teacher program may be found at www.nqaquilts.org

ETHICAL CONCERNS

There are some ethical concerns that quilt professionals must deal with. You must decide what should be done as the issues occur.

Unless you are granted written permission to do so in writing, it is not acceptable to use another person's handouts or materials. Changing that person's design by a certain amount, or copying their designs onto note cards (for example) is also a no-no. These are known as "derivative works" and are covered under copyright laws. The original designer has every right to collect damages for lost income as well as punitive damages from anyone who copies their work. There was a high profile case where several designers' works were copied and made into carpeting. The carpets were photographed by people who recognized the work and sent the photos to the original designers, who ended up pursuing the offenders in court and each getting sizable settlements.

We have already addressed some ethical concerns in the "General Chapter". Here are some additional ethical concerns.

STUDENT MACHINES

You may have all the best intentions in trying to "fix" a student's machine. Approach this with CAUTION. Students should be familiar with their machine prior to coming to class. It is helpful to always include "sewing machine manual" on your supply list whenever machines are required for a class.

You should not be taking class time to show a student how to use a new machine, or fixing a problem. It is not fair to the other students for you to take their teaching time to do machine repairs.

Merry points out that in about 90% of the cases of a contrary machine, the problem is solved by simply rethreading the machine, or pulling out and reinserting the bobbin. Another common problem can be due to a needle being inserted in the wrong position, which is especially true when students have a Singer Featherweight machine.

Consider liability issues if you do assist a student with their machine. What will happen if you break the student's machine or do further damage to it? Will the student present you with the bill for the entire machine repair?

DEMONSTRATING & SHARING SUPPLIES

Some students will be overjoyed that you choose to demonstrate with their supplies on their machine! Some will not. There are some students who are uncomfortable sharing their supplies for whatever reason, and this should be respected. You should always ASK if someone would be willing to allow you to use their "stuff" to demonstrate a technique.

You may encounter a situation where one student continuously borrows from another student or students. While most quilters are wonderful about sharing, some may feel awkward or uncomfortable doing so. You may need to tactfully interject into the situation. A good way to speak to a student individually is to approach them when they are doing their ironing, especially if there are ironing boards set up around the room. This way you are not subjecting the student to the embarrassment of speaking to them in front of a group of other students.

Weight or space limitations may prevent you from bringing "spare" supplies. Some teachers have no problem having extra supplies on hand in the event a student forgets theirs. There is always a chance that your supplies can be misplaced or accidently taken home by students, especially if the supplies are small. Merry puts her name on every piece of equipment she brings to a workshop. She often prints her name on the item with a permanent marker, and then covers it with a piece of clear tape to prevent the marker from rubbing off. This is especially helpful with rotary cutting rulers. For example, if you use an address label on a clear ruler, you will not be able to see through it.

Of course, putting your name on everything does not guarantee that it will be returned, but it certainly has a better chance of going home with you!

STUDENTS

As an educator, you should be prepared to deal with many different types of students. You will encounter needy students, "know it all" students, students whom you will never please, students with short attention spans and/or learning disabilities, and disruptive students, but for the most part you will encounter wonderful students.

You will probably want to get into the habit of making an announcement at the beginning of each class, asking students to please turn off their cell phones, or at least put them on vibrate mode. If they do get an important call, ask them to step outside of the classroom while they have their conversation. You may also wish to inform them that you may not be able to help

them catch up if you have a lot of students in the class.

GIVE 'EM MORE THAN THEY PAID FOR

Whether you are teaching at an adult education program, quilt shop, guild or show, YOU are an integral part of the student's overall experience.

Going an extra mile or two can only enhance your student's experience.

Why not include some suggestions for quilting the project (for example) or perhaps a bonus project using the scraps from the class project?

Students like bargains as much as you do, so try to give them as much "bang for the Buck" as you can.

TEACHING AT OTHER LOCAL VENUES

When you are starting to teach it doesn't hurt to let people know you are available to teach other classes or to present lectures. If quilting classes are not offered in your community, why not organize one yourself? Seek out your local Board of Education to inquire if they offer Adult Education classes.

Hourly rates from adult education classes can vary widely, from as little as $13 per hour up to $26 per hour or more. Your class will most likely be limited to students with minimal skills. This is a wonderful opportunity to be involved from the beginning with the evolution of new quilters! If you plan on working with this organization regularly, you might want to change your project each time you offer the class. Some students might form a bond and keep returning just for the fellowship. Use this opportunity to instill good quilting techniques and ethics right from the start. For example - you can discuss upcoming quilt shows - bring a quilt that you are entering - discuss the judging process and comments, perhaps even the appraisal concept - review how to complete the information for the story cards, and the process of entering a quilt in a show.

This is also a prime opportunity to educate new quilters about copyright issues. Please see our Business Issues section for more about copyrights.

These beginner quilters might very well follow you and attend classes you teach at your local shop. It also doesn't hurt to ask the shop if they will discount supplies for your students if they bring their supply lists to the shop.

Don't assume that your local adult education coordinator will understand the needs of the quilting class. You will need to explain or describe that the quilters will require large tables and adequate electrical needs. Be prepared to bring heavy-duty extension cords to class.

It is always good to have extra supplies of just about everything on your supply list for students who are unable to find the items or just forgot them. This would include basic items such as a rotary cutter, mat, and ruler, but not fabric.

OTHER LOCAL OPPORTUNITIES

Volunteering

You never know how doing something good for the world will come back to reward you later. Merry describes this as "throwing it out to the universe and see where it lands". For example, Merry volunteers her time twice per month to teach quilting at her local Gilda's Club for cancer patients, survivors, and their families. Some of these quilters have since joined us for our getaways, cruises and other activities.

Other opportunities to make presentations or teach classes may arise from historical societies, religious or social groups. Chances are pretty good that as soon as you are in the "circuit" of teaching on a local level, you will be contacted about making a presentation for THEIR group.

Be aware of budgetary issues when working with a non-profit group. Tell them what your regular rate is for presenting a lecture. Once they balk (and they will) you may wish to consider working with them and offer a slightly reduced rate, especially if it is a group you are familiar with and wish to support with your time. This decision is up to you and may depend somewhat on what kind of audience is involved.

Some groups will attempt to take advantage by offering to provide you with a free lunch or dinner in exchange for your time and expertise. Before committing to this kind of deal, be sure to consider your preparation time, travel, and time sitting through the rest of the meeting. You may also come to find out that other people have come and presented for the same group for exorbitant amounts of money.

The only time Merry teaches for free is to schools. If a group perceives you as willing to provide free programs, you may soon find yourself putting in a lot of time for free. Keep in mind your travel expenses, and time away from home, just to mention two things. Volunteering is all well and good, as long as you can afford to do it. We have found, however, that when someone pays for your services (even at a reduced rate), they take you more seriously and even tend to be more grateful that you have taken the time to speak to their group.

GETTING STARTED – Teaching at Your Local Guild

Your local quilt guild is a great place to get started in the teaching world. If guild members seem interested in the work you are showing during "show and tell", ask if they would like you to teach a class.

When you do teach for your local guild, be aware of any By-Law limits on how much guild members may be paid to teach a class or present a lecture. The rates are usually far below market rates, because you are partially volunteering your services for the benefit of the guild. In return, though, you are gaining an audience who may refer you to other local guilds, provide important feedback on your class, test your teaching ability and review your handouts. You can include the experience with this guild when you are beginning to build your resume. You can also recruit pattern testers to help you test instructions for a potential printed pattern or for further developing your techniques.

TEACHING AT A QUILT SHOP

You may be a regular customer, an accomplished quilter in your area, or a quilt professional from another area. Before you approach a shop owner or manager to discuss employment be sure that your "style" fits into the theme of that particular shop. Bring in some samples of your work, along with a sample supply list and class plans, and perhaps a copy of your resumé or portfolio. Be sure to make an appointment with the shop owner in advance.

Negotiations should include the following:

A. How does the shop pay its teachers?

a. By the hour - usually a flat fee per hour no matter how many students are in the class.

b. By the student - (ex. $20.00 per student) - the more students, the more pay you earn. Some shops pay a small additional amount per student for more than 20 students.

c. Percentage - (ex. 50% of total class fee)

d. Flat rate for full day or half day classes
   1. Shop sets the rate
   2. Teacher sets the rate

e. Teacher sets their own rate per student and the shop adds a percentage for their overhead.

There are advantages and disadvantages to each arrangement. You need to decide what is acceptable to you. Start with a lesser fee and work your way up as you gain more experience, as well as an increased reputation.

If you are paid hourly, does that include arriving early to prepare? What happens if you need to stay beyond your contracted time to help a needy student?

B. How are you paid?

a. As an employee with taxes withheld (W-9 will be required)

b. As an independent contractor (Form 1099 will be provided at the end of the year if your payment is more than $600 - this amount is set by the IRS)

C. When are you paid?

a. Within 10 days of conclusion of the class (best scenario)

b. Within 30 days of conclusion of class

c. Quarterly

d. Periodically - this should send up a red warning flag because it means that paying the teachers is not a top priority for the shop owner. They have made their profit from selling the class and any products; you are then considered to be a "vendor" and they could take six months or more to pay you.

DISCOUNTS

Does the shop offer a discount to its teachers? If so, when is the discount active? In other words, is the discount only good on days when you are teaching, or for the duration of the current issue of the newsletter? Are there exclusions to the discount, such as consignment items or gifts?

EXCLUSIVITY

Will you be "exclusive" to one shop or are you able to teach in several area shops? If the shop insists that you teach exclusively for them, what are your advantages? Will the shop pay you more to keep you there, or is it simply a "control" issue? Most shops prefer that you not teach the same class within a certain time period or within a certain area.

CLASS SAMPLE

There are no ifs, ands, or buts about it: good samples sell classes. Some shops provide fabric for a class sample at no charge. If the shop does this, please check ahead of time to see who will own the sample when the class is completed.

Some shops will require that you use the fabric they sell to make your sample. This helps them sell fabric. Some will even cut kits so they may be sold to your students. After the class is over, the kits may be offered to the shop's regular customers.

SPECIFIC OR SPECIALTY SUPPLIES

If your class requires very specific supplies that the shop does not normally stock, but you do - talk to the shop owner. Some shop owners may purchase the items from you (at cost) to sell in their shop, others may allow you to sell the products in class (perhaps splitting the profits). Remember the shop is there to make money. If you are selling things on your own, or sending students to other shops to purchase their supplies, the shop is not making money and the owner may not look kindly upon your actions.

Be considerate of the shop and try not to have numerous special supplies on your supply list.

SHOP POLICIES

Class Cancellations:

Who is responsible for notifying the teacher about class enrollment? You should contact the shop several days before your class (if the shop has not contacted you already) to determine whether your class will be a "go". If the class is cancelled, who is responsible for contacting students to notify them?

Most shops have a refund/credit policy for cancelled classes, or when students must back out of a class. Be sure the policy is included on any supply lists so the students will be aware of the policy well in advance.

Teacher Responsibilities:

Are there certain dates when teachers are permitted to sign up to teach classes for the shop's next newsletter? If so, how often can they sign up for classes? These dates usually coordinate with the publication of the shop's newsletter.

Does the teacher need to check with the shop owner to ensure that no one else will be teaching the same class?

How early is the teacher expected to arrive on the day of the class? Will the teacher be provided with a key and alarm code if they must arrive before the shop opens? Is the teacher paid for arriving early?

Who is responsible for clean up? The teacher should leave the room as clean as it was when you came in. If you are not familiar with the shop appliances, such as the vacuum, ask for a "crash course". Be familiar with the locations of the paper towels, toilet paper, and such. Always clean up after yourself, and leave the room at least as clean as you found it, if not cleaner.

Pay attention to shop merchandise and where it is located in the shop so you can take advantage of selling opportunities.

When contemplating the class you wish to teach, keep in mind the cost of the class, supplies, travel and lunch. It all adds up, and in tight economic times can influence the ability of your students to afford the luxury of taking a class.

Will the shop back you up if you have an extremely difficult student? Believe us, they are out there! Unfortunately, there are times that the difficult student may be the shop's best customer!

"NO-NO's" for Shop Teachers

- Do not "bad mouth" another teacher. Every teacher has his or her own individual style (which may or may not conform to yours). Some students will relate better to one teacher or another. Gossiping or belittling another teacher can only cause friction, and will ultimately backfire on you.

- It is in very poor taste to discuss what is on sale at another shop while you are teaching. You should also not discuss what you are teaching at other shops. You are teaching in **THIS** shop and you are there to promote **THIS** shop. You should do your best to re-direct student conversations about other shops while you are teaching.

- Do not discuss any personal, political or religious issues. You should also try to re-direct any student conversations away from these issues.

- Do your best to keep your students "on task". Too much conversation could result in one or more students not completing the project. Furthermore, you could end up staying to help them catch up.

- If you are privy to certain shop issues (such as problems between employees, etc.) it is very unprofessional for you to share these with your students.

- Do NOT talk about one student or customer to another.

FOR MORE INFORMATION

Be sure to check our Resources section for information on organizations that are geared toward professionals in the quilting industry, such as the Quilt Professionals' Network. There is also an excellent quarterly magazine, The Professional Quilter, which has articles specifically targeting people who are either already in the industry, or who are considering joining the industry.

HITTING THE ROAD

Traveling to teach is not as glamorous as people may think. It can be a lot of fun, but it is a lot of hard work. We often hear guild program chairs talking about how expensive it is to bring in a teacher. They do not take into consideration the prep time, which includes making samples, writing supply lists, making up handouts, printing costs, travel time, or waiting time (for example, at the airport or while the guild has a meeting before you speak).

What you are entitled to:
- Your fee
- Round trip mileage at current IRS rates; go to IRS.gov for the most current rate
- Round trip airfare plus ground

transportation to and from your home to the airport as well as to and from the teaching location; once you build up some frequent flyer miles, you can use them to upgrade to a first class seat. Do not expect a guild to pay for this!
- Reimbursement of airport parking, highway tolls
- Meals (door to door or per diem)
- Hotel/Motel/B&B or Hosted Stay with the possibility of an extra night before or after the teaching time to allow for travel.
- Reimbursement of copying costs (if applicable and spelled out in your contract)

In the Forms section of this book, you will find several different teaching contracts and expense sheets. You are welcome to extract parts from any of them to create a contract to suit your own needs.
Here are a few things to think about:

- You are NOT obligated to stay at a member's home if you do not want to. There are some teachers who prefer to stay with a guild member and there are those who appreciate the "down time" a hotel affords. Almost every guild will ask you to stay in a member's home to save costs. Do not feel compelled to do this just because it is requested.

- It is imperative that you get a second guild person's contact information, and especially a cell phone number so you can reach someone while you are on your way to the venue. Program chairs and presidents may change from the time you are booked to the time you actually arrive. It is always a good idea to speak to someone on the telephone a few days in advance of your visit just to touch base and reconfirm everything.

- If someone is meeting you at the airport, be sure they have a vehicle capable of handling your luggage. By the way, how strong are you? Do not depend on someone else to help you to move/lift your luggage.

- If you have things to sell at your presentation, be sure to clear it with the guild first and get it in writing. More and more guilds are asking for a percentage of the sales. If the guild asks for a percentage, explain that the profit from the sales keeps your fees lower for the guild. Perhaps you could offer to donate a door prize. You are responsible for the costs of getting your "stuff" to and from the location.

- It doesn't hurt to give the program person a little thank you gift (perhaps one of your patterns). A thank you note or e-mail to the program person after the presentation is also recommended.

  Many guilds are becoming more considerate of teacher waiting time. Having a speaker at the meeting is not the time to have your major quilt show meeting with the guild. It doesn't hurt to ask if you can present your program before the meeting, even if you are staying over.

- When traveling long distances with more than one suitcase, pack some of your quilts in one bag, and the rest of your quilts in a second bag. This way in case one suitcase is lost or damaged, you won't lose everything. It is always a good idea to carry your lecture or workshop notes with you, along with any necessary handouts.

- You were hired to teach - not to promote your "stuff". Make your pertinent items available, but don't waste the guild's money for you to present your "infomercial". You can always ask for a volunteer to handle sales for you (perhaps gift them with a pattern or special something as a thank you).

- There are times when you may be asked to teach in less than ideal or uncomfortable locations. You can ask the program person in advance if there is air conditioning or heat so you can dress appropriately. No matter what the circumstances, do your best to "go with the flow" and be a good sport if something happens to go wrong. More than one teacher has not been invited back to teach because they were too demanding, or considered to be prima donnas.

- If you are asked to shorten your presentation, be sure to make it clear to your audience that you were asked to do so, but do it politely. A program person from another guild or future program person may be in the audience. If they don't know that you were ASKED to shorten your program, they may think poorly of you.

- This is not the time to indulge in the consumption of alcoholic beverages. A glass of wine with dinner might be fine, but you need to look at yourself from other people's perspective. Merry always sticks with plain old water at dinner. Other beverages sometimes can cause allergic reactions or post-nasal drip leading to a less than ideal presentation.

- This is also not the time to discuss your divorce, personal problems, views on politics or controversial issues. Keep your language rated at "G" or "PG" whenever possible, especially if you see young people in the audience. Unless everyone in attendance is aware that you include "colorful" language in your presentation, there could be a number of people who are offended. On the other hand, there are speakers who are wildly popular because they do use colorful language, and talk about topics that you don't normally hear about at guild meetings. There are teaching "gigs" for just about anyone, and on almost any topic!

- Some teachers will have evaluation forms for students to complete after their workshop. Evaluations should be carefully read and you should be objective when doing so. If you ask specific questions on your evaluation form, you will be better able to pinpoint your strengths and weaknesses.

- When offering a new workshop or lecture, you may want to consider offering it to a local guild for free or at a reduced rate. You should announce at the beginning that this is a "test" and ask for feedback after the presentation.

- You may be asked to dine with the program chair or members of the guild's board. Show some consideration for their expenses; this is not the time to order lobster.

- Please remember your own personal hygiene. Try not to wear perfume; many people are allergic to it, or have respiratory problems which are triggered by it.

- You will find that there are some guilds who are very considerate to teachers, and some who are not. When you check into your hotel, you may discover a small gift waiting for you. This may consist of a pretty bag containing some water, snacks, chocolate and contact numbers for the appropriate guild people. Some bags even contain directions to local malls, hotels, movie timetables and local coupons.

- You should always try to have some extra supplies for workshops on hand for those who forgot theirs; for example, an extra ruler, mat or rotary cutter. This may not be possible for teachers who are flying and space/weight is at a premium.

SUPPLY LISTS

Your supply list should be clear and concise. Think back to some of the classes you have taken - has there not been a student who stated they didn't know to bring a 1/4" foot or scissors? See our Forms section for some supply list samples.

One of the biggest complaints about supply lists is that some may contain supplies that the students end up not using in class. Others complain that it is difficult to find some specialty supplies. We suggest that you have optional supplies or perhaps a notation that the optional supplies might be available for purchase at the workshop. We often bring extras of any special tools to share with our students.

TEACHER EVALUATION GROUPS

Be aware that there are several quilt guild networking groups around the country. During the year, guild program chairs get together and share their opinions on teachers, programs and other quilt professionals. They also compare notes on things like insurance, mixers, how they handle memberships, and many other things.

We just want you to be aware that each group has their own rules about what may or may not be said about teachers who are registered with the group as a resource. Some groups allow people to speak freely and with anonymity, but refrain from putting any of the comments in writing. Some put the comments in writing and distribute them amongst the attendees in the form of Minutes after the meeting. There are legitimate concerns about libel and slander. For example, two teachers may have similar names - one may be a "good" teacher and the other is "not so good". What if one of the networking members mixes up the teachers and makes disparaging remarks about the "good" teacher? If other guilds then decide not to hire the "good" teacher because of the remarks, then this could become a legal issue because the teacher is losing the ability to earn her living, not to mention her reputation. This can happen.

Networking groups need to be very cautious when evaluating teachers or other professionals. Evaluating is all well and good but those who are making the comments need to be certain about who they are evaluating, and also the evaluations should be provided with objectivity. As an example - YOU do not like art quilts - Jane Doe did a presentation on art quilts - she did not hold your attention because you do not like art quilts - but was she a good speaker despite your not being personally interested in the subject?

One way for these groups to avoid subjecting themselves to liability is to provide written evaluation forms to the program chairs, and ask the program chairs to send in their completed evaluations within 60 days of when the program was presented. This way the information is still relatively fresh in the evaluator's mind, and they will at least be able to get the name of the presenter correct. A copy of the evaluation could also be mailed to the teacher. When the networking group has their meeting, the evaluations can be summarized by the leader of the group, and then be shared with the members. If the teacher ultimately has a question about the evaluation, he or she should have the opportunity to dispute it or at least comment on it. After all, even suspected criminals have the opportunity to face their accusers, professionals should certainly be afforded the same right.

TEACHING AT A SHOW

At some point in your teaching career, you may wish to try teaching at a quilt show. The show teaching environment is different than teaching at a shop. You should be prepared to teach up to 25 students, of all different skill levels. This is because shop personnel may be able to effectively screen the skill levels of students prior to class, while shows do not have this opportunity. You need to be able to effectively communicate your instructions in several different ways to accommodate the different learning abilities — and sometimes learning disabilities - of the students.

Teachers who teach at a show are also expected to exhibit the highest standards of professionalism. Dress appropriately, and be sure you look your best. Remember that regardless of what else is going on in your life (other than true family emergencies), "the show – or in this case, the class - must go on."

Show Managers may seek out a particular teacher based on his or her current popularity, or perhaps even how the teacher's class offerings will fit into the current trend or theme of the show. Show Managers also receive teaching credentials on almost a daily basis from teachers wishing to be considered for a position. Show Managers are always on the lookout for new or emerging faces in the industry.

We suggest that you have several presentations (whole and half day offerings) for the Show Manager to choose from. In all likelihood they will hire you for more than one class because it is more cost effective for them.

Your proposals should include the skill level for each workshop, whether it is a class that may be done by hand or if it requires a machine; supply list; any additional costs to students (such as for a pattern); and a photo of the project.

If you are invited by a Show Manager to teach, you should promptly provide them with your short bio, photograph, supply lists and whatever else they request from you.

The Show Manager will provide you with instructions on how to ship classroom items (at your own expense) if necessary, hotel information, directions, and perhaps an invitation to a dinner, luncheon or other special show events.

When you arrive at the show, you should check in to the hotel and if possible visit your classroom so you are familiar with the location. You should also check in with show staff so they are aware that

you have safely arrived. Some shows will provide you with an attendance list prior to class.

Arrive at your classroom early enough so you can get set up prior to your students arriving. This will enable you to greet the students as they arrive.

During the lunch break, if you have occasion to walk through any area of the show, be prepared to be stopped and perhaps asked for an autograph or photo opportunity. Be gracious, patient and humble, but appreciative of the recognition. You are a very important part of the quilter's show experience. Some quilters will be absolutely afraid to even come near you, some will just stare and others will approach you just to say hello and are excited to have spoken to a "celebrity". We've even observed a table of quilters become ecstatic when a teacher asked to join some students and their friends to eat lunch. Most quilters will not approach you when you are in the middle of a meal.

When fellow teacher, Mark Lipinski, walks through a show, at times you might think you are at a rock concert. He is constantly swarmed by quilters for a hug, kiss, autograph or joke! After he has gone, you will hear quilters telling their friends that they "met Mark" and you can also read postings on e-mail discussion lists and blogs about their meetings with Mark. Mark takes it all in stride and even though he may be hot, thirsty or hungry, he goes out of his way to ensure that all who want to meet him do so.

When you have completed your teaching assignment, seek out the Show Manager and turn in your expense sheet. Be sure to thank the Show Manager for inviting you.

Most shows will forward your per diem meal allowance prior to the show. The range for a per diem is between $25 and $35 per day. Travel expenses (if not paid by the show directly) and your fees will be forwarded to you shortly after the show.

There are several large shows which do not pay their teachers at all. These teachers may be vendors or sponsored by a company. Some shows may pay all teachers the same rate, while others will pay only a portion of the expenses. Be sure to read your contract carefully before signing and returning it, even though you may be very excited to be invited to teach at this venue.

One of the most important things to remember as a teacher is that, although you are in the spotlight, being kind and humble both go a long way in contributing to your success. Merry's view is that, as soon as she steps out of line, God will strike her down (and He does!). So don't let a little notoriety go to your head. Remember your humble beginnings, and offer a helping hand to others who are trying to learn the ropes.

Chapter Four
Retreats and Cruises

Retreats and Getaways are becoming more and more popular with quilters. They are a chance to get away for a day or so (and sometimes even more) and quilt with your friends. Quilting cruises have also risen in popularity but it is more difficult to coordinate a cruise than it is a Retreat or Getaway. Cruises are obviously more costly for the quilter to participate in.

The income potential for a retreat or getaway (which we will collectively refer to as "retreats" in this chapter) can vary greatly and will depend on several factors which we will cover in this chapter.

1. The Facility or Venue

Finding a suitable place to accommodate your group is the first thing you must address before deciding on dates, how many quilters you can accept, or anything else.

Do you want to hold your retreat in a Bed & Breakfast type of environment, or at a hotel? In a B&B, you may be very limited as to the number of attendees that the individual location can accommodate. In a hotel type of environment, you are limited to the number of participants that you can effectively teach. What is the cost for each room beyond the standard double occupancy (for example, a triple or a quad)? What about commuters: people who want to participate, but live nearby and don't want to stay with the group? What are the amenities in each room? Is the location accessible to people with disabilities? Can it handle the electrical needs of the group? Are you required to guarantee a certain number of rooms to the venue? How much of a deposit do they require?

Do you have to pay extra for the area where the quilting activities will take place, such as a conference room, or is that included with the commitment for a certain number of rooms? If there is a cost, obviously that needs to be factored into the retreat pricing.

2. The Food

Does your venue offer rates which include meals (for example, breakfast)? If not, you need to decide whether you want to provide meals for your attendees or if they will be "on their own" for meals. If you are providing the meals, then the cost of each meal must be factored into the cost of the retreat. You might contact a local restaurant to see if you can make arrangements with them to bring your group in for a meal, or, if there is enough space at your venue, maybe look into having one or more meals catered. If you go to a restaurant, you may be asked to commit to a specific time (probably not at their peak dining times) and perhaps be limited to specific choices from the menu. You will most likely need to send them a deposit in advance. Be sure to ask if they will accept a check from you on the day of your group's visit.

If you are at a Bed & Breakfast, you will most likely be able to bring in some wine, cheese and finger foods for your attendees to munch on while quilting. In the hotel situation, you might be able to order some goodies (for a fee), but you also may be able to bring in some cookies, cakes, wine and cheese. It's always a good idea to have some snacks on hand. We have found that many of our quilters also prefer to have bottled water available. We usually purchase 2 or 3 cases of small bottles of water for our 30 quilters for our weekends. Once again, figure the cost of the various items into the price of the retreat, including any paper goods.

Dining arrangements (as we have discussed above) and times should be strictly adhered to. If you have a 4:30 reservation, it is best to have your quilters stop at 4:00 to prepare for dinner. If it is necessary to drive to the restaurant, try to have everyone carpool to the location, and make sure the drivers have good directions!

3. The Classes

For the most part, you will not know the skill levels of the people signing up for your retreat. Over time, you will be able to ascertain what type of classes will work for your retreat. Keep in mind that there are some who like to learn a technique, and there are some who like to bring home a completed project. If you work with a partner, as Linda and Merry do, you will be able to offer a larger variety of classes; perhaps one can be more advanced than the other. You should provide a skill level for each class you offer, as well as a definition of what each skill level means. See our web site at Double Trouble Studios (www.DoubleTroubleStudios.com) for a link to our downloadable "BBQ" (Bed, Breakfast & Quilt) Registration packet, so you can see how we do this. This is also included in the "Forms" section of this book.

We also offer the option of bringing the retreaters' own projects to work on rather than taking a class. Many of our quilters choose to take an all-day class on Saturday, and then continue working on that project on Sunday, rather than starting on a second project.

4. Kits & Supplies

Coordinated and pre-cut kits that are offered as an optional purchase are usually welcomed by your quilters. You can make some additional income by offering these kits. It is suggested that you offer the opportunity to pre-order them so that you do not go to the unnecessary expense of purchasing supplies and cutting kits that you will not need. We usually bring at least a couple of extra kits for people who may decide they want them after they arrive for the weekend.

It is very important that your attendees be provided with accurate supply lists. You should also be very clear about what is included in any kits you are selling, and the cost for any patterns or books they may be required to purchase. We often offer a small discount for those who pre-order any books, patterns or kits from us.

5. Door Prizes

It's always fun to win a door prize! If you are able to purchase wholesale, you can purchase some door prizes to give away. Allow a certain dollar amount per person, but then split up the values of the prizes so some are worth more than others. You could include anything from thread to fat quarters to books, and anything in between.

A note about door prize donation requests: As small business owners, we are all too familiar with organizers of retreats, guild shows and shop hops who contact businesses requesting donations to give away as door prizes.

We want you to know that, if you place any kind of advertisements in any publications, you are subject to being bombarded with these requests on an almost daily basis. If you are a small business owner, you eventually come to the conclusion that if you donate to everyone who makes a request (and some are not even legitimate, believe it or not!), you will soon be out of business. Over the years we have found ways to filter out some of the excessive requests. One is to set a donation budget each year, keep track of how much you are giving away, and say no when you reach your limit. Another is to only donate to local guilds whose members are more likely to actually be customers who support your own business. After awhile, you get to the point where you just don't even respond to the requests. It costs you both time and postage just to politely say no. One of Merry's pet peeves when she had a toll-free telephone number was when people would call her on the toll-free number to ask for donations. It was costing her money for them to ask for handouts!

Anyway, we think you get the idea. Be considerate of small business owners and their bottom lines before asking for them to contribute to your bottom line.

That being said, here are three different ways that we use to choose the door prize winners at our retreats:

- Have everyone put their name tag in a bag, and randomly draw the name tags; when your name tag is chosen, it's your turn to go pick out a door prize.

- Ask the quilters to introduce themselves one at a time. Once they have introduced themselves, they may then go choose a door prize. One way to cut down on the distractions is to hand each person a number as they do their introduction, and have them go choose their prize in turn once everyone has been introduced.

- Use stickers to number each door prize. Then make up a duplicate set of numbers on slips of paper. Put the numbered papers into a bag, and have each quilter draw a number. The number they choose corresponds with the number on one of the door prizes.

6. The Schedule

Provide your attendees with a clear schedule of activities and adhere to it.

Quilters seem to automatically bond, although there are some who can be newbies, single attendees or just plain shy. An ice-breaker or "mixer" could help your attendees get to know each other.

One way to get everyone to mix and meet is to have each person choose someone they don't know. Give them 5 minutes to chat and try to find something they have in common (other than quilting, if possible). Then have everyone introduce their new friend to the rest of the group.

Name tags are another way to encourage people to get to know each other. Some people really dislike wearing them, but it sure beats addressing each other as "hey, you!"

7. Evaluations

A well-thought-out evaluation sheet can help you gather information to make your next retreat even more successful (see our sample in Forms). Although some comments may hurt (ask us how we know), you need to use them to determine what your customers' expectations are. At the same time, you may have an attendee who had a misunderstanding of what the retreat was all about, or even someone who will not be happy no matter WHAT you do. They're out there. Use the evaluations as constructive criticism to improve the retreat experience for your customers.

8. Advertising

How are you going to start a customer base? Professional looking flyers need to be printed and possibly mailed. They can be left at quilt shops and quilt shows and also mailed to quilt guilds. If you do lectures or workshops for other guilds you can bring a stack of them to distribute; if the guild members enjoy your program they will be more likely to sign up to spend a weekend with you. The cost of the printing and mailing will be deducted from your profits.

Our Bed, Breakfast & Quilt ("BBQ") Getaways, which we offer twice per year, have grown considerably to the point where we no longer need to advertise as aggressively. We have many repeat customers who have become good friends. They in turn spread the word about how much fun they had, which encourages others to join us as well. The current attendees are always offered the first opportunity to sign up for the next BBQ. We also offer a $10 discount for being "early birds," encouraging them to give us their deposits for the next BBQ. We give them about a month to do this, so they do not feel pressured to sign up before they leave the current BBQ retreat. We do accept credit cards, and we will cover this issue in our Business Issues section.

9. Other Issues
Refunds

Make up a Refund Policy and be sure to make it clear on the registration form (see Forms for a sample of one of our BBQ schedules). Furthermore, you need to stick to your policy. There should be some amount of the deposit that is non-refundable to cover your fixed expenses like advertising and the mailings you have done. You have held that spot and may have lost the opportunity to fill it. Admittedly, though, there have been extenuating circumstances when we provided partial refunds, such as in the event of a family emergency. We consider this to be a goodwill gesture, encouraging the person to sign up with us on another occasion. Regardless of how much money you need to refund, be sure to send the check out promptly, and include a note saying you hope they will join you for a future getaway.

We have also rolled over deposits from one BBQ to the next one, but will only do this once, again as a goodwill gesture. Otherwise you could end up rolling over deposits and holding rooms for no-shows forever.

Machines

If you are comfortable and confident in your knowledge, you may offer to assist someone having difficulty with their machine. Be aware that you may be held responsible if you break something. It has happened. A well meaning teacher attempted to help a student with her machine, and was unsuccessful. The student presented her with the bill from the machine repairman claiming that her attempt to fix the machine made it worse which necessitated a trip to the repair shop.

Roommates

You may encounter some single quilters who desire to save a little money and room with another quilter. You can offer to put that quilter in touch with another single quilter and they can decide between themselves whether they wish to room together.

Teacher Time

You need to determine the time you will actually be TEACHING and the time you are "available". They are two different things. Some of the attendees will stay up all night or even all weekend. You obviously cannot do that. Be sure to announce that you will be "retiring" to your room for the evening, and ask for

a volunteer to be sure the lights are out, ceiling fans are off, extension cords (and especially the irons!) are all unplugged, food has been put away, and the doors are locked. Usually you do not need to leave a key; you just need to show the volunteer how to lock the doors.

Calculating the Costs

How do you decide how much to charge each person for your getaway? Charge too little and you don't make much money; charge too much, and people will balk at the price.

Expenses obviously will vary depending on what part of the country you are in, and what time of year it is. People who live in resort areas will want to schedule their getaways during off-peak times whenever possible, in order to get the best rates for hotels or B&Bs. However, you also do not want to schedule your getaway at a time of year when you are likely to run into bad weather (like during the winter in the northern US!).

We are providing a chart below as an example of things to consider when making this important decision. Fees are per person in the chart, and are based on a group of 30 paying participants.

	Expenses	Single	Double	Triple	Quad & Up	Commuter
Room (double occ. rate)	$200	$200	$100	$66.67	$50	N/a
Add'l room fee per person	$40	N/a	N/a	$40	$40	$30 charged by hotel
Meal(s) Per person	$30	$30	$30	$30	$30	$30
Door Prizes Per person	$10	$10	$10	$10	$10	$10
Snacks*	$150	$5	$5	$5	$5	$10
Advertising*	$150	$5	$5	$5	$5	$10
Costs for Your Own Room, Meals, etc.*	$250	$10	$10	$10	$10	$10
Professional Fee per Student**	$50	$50	$50	$50	$50	$50
Cost Per Person		$310	$210	$216.67	$200	$150
Fee Per Person***		$360	$260	$240	$220	$170
Projected Net Profit per Person		$50	$50	$23.33	$20	$20

* "Snacks," "Advertising" and the "Cost for Your Own Room & Meals" are shown at their full rate in the Expenses column, but are then divided by 30 (number of participants) for the remaining columns. "Snacks" includes paper goods, wine, cheese, and other foods. "Advertising" includes all mailings and printing expenses. For Double Occupancy rooms and above, the Double Occupancy rate is divided equally among the number of people in the room.

** "Professional Fee per Student" compensates you for your services as a teacher. If there are two teachers, the fee is split equally.

*** "Fee Per Person" reflects anticipated increases in Room and Meal fees, postage, printing, snacks, insurance, net profit, and any unexpected expenses.

After reviewing the above chart, you will see that the host of the above scenario works pretty cheaply. She is compensated for her teaching time, but the net profits are quite modest. You may wish to start out at a low rate of return and then gradually increase the fees as you gain a loyal customer base.

Bookkeeping and Registrar Duties

Keeping an accurate accounting of deposits, and sending out confirmations and reminders is an important part of organizing a retreat. Be sure to mark on your calendar when mailings need to be sent out. For example, we always try to do a mailing with a final accounting of deposits, classes and roommates about two weeks before final payments are due. We also include a list of dinner choices for Saturday's dinner, and ask them to call us with their selection. If the person has already paid in full, we add a personal "thank you" to their statement. This is also when we send the directions to the hotel, a discount coupon from the local quilt shop, and any other necessary reminders.

Don't Forget

One of the most important things to remember when you are in the throes of a weekend retreat is to be yourself, and have a good time. Your own enthusiasm will rub off on others and they will relax and enjoy themselves, too.

CRUISES

Cruises are not something that you can run entirely on your own. You need the services and advice of a travel professional, preferably one who does group tours and cruises on a regular basis so they are familiar with the ins and outs of the cruising industry.

A larger agency is most likely experienced in working with groups that have special requirements. They are also able to invest more in advertising. The larger agency may have an established relationship with the cruise line and thus may be able to offer more "perks" to the group, such as a get-together cocktail party.

The travel agency may be able to make arrangements to bring the quilters to the pier via buses. The buses will make stops along the way to pick up quilters, their machines and luggage.

Consideration should be given to the projects you offer. People want to know what projects are being offered, and will also want to see photos and have their supply lists ready when they sign up for the cruise. The classes should appeal to all skill levels because, again, you will be working with both experienced and inexperienced quilters. The same suggestions we offered under Retreats for kits would apply to cruises.

Pricing should be considered, as well as the time of year, especially along the eastern coast of the US during hurricane season. In addition, you should be aware of the age of the people in your group, and try to make accommodations as easy as possible for them. For example, often Linda's husband serves as a "bellhop" for the ladies in our groups, helping them to transport their machines and supplies from their cabins to the classroom and back.

We use the word "classroom" very loosely here, because most ships do not have conference rooms, let alone classrooms. When they do have extra public spaces, they often have art auctions going on or other events which prevent you from using them. As a result, we have taught most of our classes in the ships' dining rooms during the day when they are not being used. This means that the tables are at dining table height, which can be a little high when you have a sewing machine on top of them. We have also worked in areas where there are booths rather than tables with separate chairs. The lighting in the ship's dining room is often not very good, so this is another area where you may encounter some difficulties. You also must work around the dining room's schedule, which can result in some odd class schedules.

Quilting classes are usually only held on sea days. Any days in port are spent on your own, and the other people in your group are expected to do likewise.

Machines may or may not be provided. There may be a local machine dealer who is interested in providing machines for the quilting cruise in exchange for sending their representative along as a machine monitor and salesperson. If quilters are asked to bring their machines, they should know the make, model and wattage for their machine. This is because the cruise line manufactures its own electricity and must prepare for the extra electricity required by many machines. There are also customs forms to be completed for the machines.

Irons are generally prohibited onboard a ship, or are only "legal" when used in fireproof laundry room areas. Be sure to inform the travel agent well in advance about how many irons your group will be using. We try to limit ourselves to only two or three irons for the entire group. Of course this sometimes results in long lines of students waiting for their turn to use an iron, but it is beyond your control. Once you explain this to the students, they are usually pretty understanding about it.

Cruises are actually a little bit easier on you than retreats, because the travel agent who accompanies you is expected to deal with all of the details in regards to getting everyone moved in and out, and any problems with the rooms, meals, and such. However, do not depend completely on the travel agent to handle these; it is quite possible that someone could be injured when the travel agent is off doing their own thing. You need to know how to handle the situation, and who to contact onboard the ship.

Something else you need to consider is that you are expected to be "on" every minute of the cruise, so if one of your group members sees you when classes are not in session, you need to be friendly, helpful and accessible. Be sure to dress appropriately, even when you are not teaching classes; remember, you are the "star" of the group, so you need to act accordingly.

Most groups arrange to have their evening meals together so they can all visit and compare stories about how their day was. This is one of the main reasons people sign up for quilting cruises; so they can mingle with other people who share the same interests. It is also a good opportunity to make any necessary announcements while going from table to table to greet everyone.

Teachers may work in exchange for the "cabin" (which is normally double occupancy), or they may be paid as if they were teaching at a guild or show. The arrangement with the teaching staff is negotiable.

Chapter Five
Longarm Quilting

Machine quilting can be broken down into three categories: Domestic (the same sewing machine on which you pieced the top), Mid Arm - a light duty long arm machine usually purchased by the quilter for their own use, and Long Arm – an industrial machine usually purchased to quilt for others.

Almost all quilters today are familiar with long arm machine quilting. Providing this service for quilters is getting more and more popular. Long arm machine quilting offers quilters the opportunity to have the quilting done for them (and sometimes even the binding, sleeve and label) so that they receive a completely finished quilt back.

Quilt shows are recognizing and accepting quilts which have been long arm machine quilted. Judges are becoming familiar with the judging criteria specific to the long arm machine quilted quilt in addition to the quilt which was quilted on a domestic machine.

This is an area where you can, in fact, quit your day job. The amount of money you can make depends on how hard you want to work. This can run the gamut up to $50,000 +/- per year. YOU are responsible for not only promoting and operating an honest, professional, customer oriented business but also for safeguarding your customers' precious quilts while they are in your custody.

You cannot just purchase a long arm machine and think that customers are going to be knocking each other over to have their quilts quilted by you. You not only must invest a lot of money, but also a lot of time and energy before that first dollar changes hands. You will most likely not be seeing any type of profit for at least a year, considering your start up costs of machine purchase, training, threads, batting, advertisements, and the like.

Please refer to the other chapters in the book which deal with setting up your business entity, checking account, securing a business license, any zoning requirements for your neighborhood, insurance, and any sales tax requirements.

PURCHASING THE MACHINE

There are so many machines available on the market today. The differences range from the size of quilt the machine can accommodate to the color of the machine. This is going to be your most important purchase, so it is imperative that you do your homework. First and foremost is: how much can you afford to spend? There are machines that will fit into almost any budget. Speak to other long arm quilters to see what they like or dislike about their machines. Take measurements of the room where you intend to put your machine so you are not surprised when the machine is delivered and does not fit!

Usually the larger quilt shows will have several mid arm dealers and long arm machine dealers available in the vendor mall. One of the best places to test drive almost every machine available at one time is at one of the quilt shows geared specifically for machine quilters.

Take your time and test drive the machine before you buy it. Ask lots of questions, such as about repair services, training, and other resources you may need to know about. This piece of machinery will, in essence, be your business partner.

Each machine has certain bells and whistles specific to that machine which make it unique. Some machines offer computer guided models. A stitch regulator is now offered on almost all machine models. The table for the machine varies according to the make and model you choose. The longest table is 14 feet long and can accommodate a large king size quilt.

The price for long arm machines vary, and will depend on the size, construction of the machine (aluminum or steel), add-ons (such as auto-advance, thread cutter, stitch regulator, etc). Smaller machines can start at $5000 and then go upwards from there. Several companies offer the opportunity to upgrade your machine with an add-on computer guidance system. Depending on the system you choose, you will be adding an additional $7,000-$15,000 to the cost of your machine.

PREPARING THE LONG ARM STUDIO

You need to ask yourself the following questions when you are designing your studio.

- Where and how will the quilts be stored that are waiting to be quilted? They must be kept in a clean, dry place.

- Where and how will the quilts that are completed be stored until they are picked up? Quilts should be bagged in a muslin storage bag, or a clear plastic bag. Some people use plastic hangers and dry cleaner bags. They should be kept clean and neatly folded until claimed by their owner.

- How will I store my threads? Threads need to be kept clean and away from direct sunlight to avoid fading and dry rot. Some quilters will place their threads on wall racks (covered with a sheet or plastic protector), some may use large plastic containers.

- Will customers be coming into your studio? If so, do you have a place for them to sit?

- What type of flooring will you have? You might consider an anti-fatigue mat on top of a tile floor to make cleaning easier.

- What are your lighting needs? You may need to add additional lighting.

- How will the customers enter and exit your studio? Is the sidewalk safe?

- Are there stairs to negotiate? You may need to make some improvements so your customers can get in and out of your studio safely and easily.

- Will you be offering batting for sale? If so, how will you store it?

- Do you have bathroom facilities easily accessible to your studio so your customers do not have to venture through the house?

INITIAL INVESTMENT

Aside from the machine purchase, you may (or may not) need to do some renovations to your long arm studio to accommodate your machine. These renovations might include new flooring or lighting. You will also need to invest in threads. Don't skimp on quality or quantity of thread. If you are unable to purchase a lot of thread initially, you may want to invest in the color cards that contain actual thread. These cards can be purchased through a wholesale distributor. Some machine dealers will provide you with several cones of thread, a roll or two of batting and some simple pantographs to get you started.

Will you be offering batting for your customers to purchase? Doing so may generate some extra income for you if you purchase the batting wholesale. While it may not appear to make a difference on a quilt by quilt basis, you may see several

hundred dollars come your way by the end of the month. It would be wise to have some batting swatches and perhaps even a quilt available for your customers to feel so they can decide which batting they might wish to use.

Batting can be purchased wholesale through distributors (please see our Resource section) in either rolls or packaged. You need to decide whether it is more cost effective for your business to offer batting from the roll or packaged.

Here is a low estimate of initial start up costs:

Machine purchase
$15,000.00
Sales tax & delivery charge
$ 500.00
Room renovation (by handy spouse)
$ 2,500.00
Thread (basic colors - wholesale)
$ 260.00
Batting (roll - wholesale)
$ 150.00
Advertising budget (first year)
$ 250.00
Printing costs (business cards, brochures)
$ 200.00

Don't forget to save your receipts for any changes or improvements you make to your house to give to your tax professional at the end of the year.

ADVERTISEMENTS

You will need professional business cards. You don't want to hand out home printed business cards that have the nubs left on the card edges. This is very unprofessional.

Business cards are not that expensive to have printed. Check your local office supply store for pricing.

You will also need a brochure that tells about you and what you do. The brochure can be left at quilt shows, quilt shops and guild meetings. If you leave one panel blank, why not make it suitable for mailing? There are some desktop publishing programs that offer templates to make the design of your brochure simple. Once you have established yourself, you may want to invest in professionally made brochures printed on a heavier paper.

Before you start placing ads, think about where your clients will come from. When you are first starting out, your clientele would most likely be friends and local quilters. You may want to consider an ad in your local guild newsletter.

As your business grows, you will need to re-visit the advertising budget. Word of mouth from happy customers is always the best form of advertisement. There are numerous long arm quilters who indicated they were able to stop advertising altogether after being in business for a few years.

An inexpensive way of advertising is to enter your quilts in local quilt shows. You can either enter your own quilts - and be sure to include your business name as the quilter (with your name in parenthesis) or you can do some quilts for friends and ask them to enter them in shows. Be sure to ask them to include your business name on their entry form, showing that you were the one who did the quilting for them.

If you are a teacher, you can quilt your class sample and then provide each student with a coupon for a dollar amount or percentage off of the fee for quilting the top they just made in your class.

The best advertisement you can have is a happy customer!

SOFTWARE FOR LONGARMERS

You may want to consider long arm-specific software to help you manage your business. At the present time, there are two software programs available:

"Quilters Business Suite" (QBS) and "Machine Quilter's Business Manager" (MQBM). Please refer to the Resources section for where to purchase each of these programs.

Both programs are Windows based. If you own a Mac, you will need to have an additional program that enables you to open Windows based programs.

QBS has a free demo version available for download at www.f2innovations.com. Todd Fletcher, developer of the "QBS" software is a "computer geek" and provides great customer service.

Both programs provide comprehensive manuals in addition to the disk and are priced in the range of $150.00.

These programs each allow you to maintain a customer database, manage your wait list, generate reports on taxes, inventory (thread, batting, etc) and also print custom invoices.

Mary Reinhart, developer of the "MQBM" software offers classes for both beginner and advanced "MQBM" users at the larger machine quilting shows.

CUSTOMER SERVICE

As a long arm quilter, you will need to deal with many different types and personalities of customers.

There are some customers who are

very happy to give you their quilt top and backing fabric and leave the rest up to you. There are also customers who wish to control the entire process and will not listen to any recommendations you may make, and there are those who fall in between.

The Controller has a picture in his or her mind what the quilt is supposed to look like when it is done. This may or may not be what is best suited for this particular quilt. Nothing you suggest or recommend will be considered. This person will most likely not acknowledge any piecing or construction inaccuracies that might contribute to the end result of the quilt. Because of this, you need to document this quilt extremely carefully as well as any requests the customer may have. Take photos if necessary. Depending on the customer, you may even choose to write down "customer insisted on so and so". This customer may or may not be happy with the end result.

You could also run into Miss Two Tons of Tops. Two Tons may be the speed racer of the quilt world and the construction of her tops reflect this. You may find holes in seam allowances, mismatched seams, borders that were not measured before application (get the picture?). Miss Two Tons could most likely become a very good customer. She may or may not be open to some helpful suggestions. You must remember that you are NOT a quilt judge; however, you can use some carefully chosen words to educate your customer on how to provide you with better tops which will, in turn, become better quilts to return to her. In the Forms section, you will find an information sheet which Linda encloses with each quilt return.

Bargain Betty may also find her way to your studio door. Betty will bring you a

top constructed of the fabrics she found in grandma's attic (which could be of any blend or weave), and a bag of batting that pulls apart like cotton candy which she purchased on clearance at the local chain store along with $0.89 per yard muslin for the back. The borders are not measured and she wants to be able to fold the backing over for the binding. She wants the cheapest possible design. She is not the least bit interested in paying you the extra charges for clipping threads, re-attaching the borders, using a good quality batting and applying a decent binding. Most likely your instructions will be "just quilt it as it is."

CUSTOMER SERVICE TIPS

If you feel uncomfortable doing what the customer asks you to do, you can let them know that you will do the work their way, but you will not guarantee your work – and be sure to put it in writing. This is usually enough to make them think twice. You are allowed to say "NO" and you can reserve the right not to accept any quilt.

If you cannot do what the customer asks, it is important that you tell them that you do not know how to execute that particular request. Do not accept the quilt just to get work. It is more important for you to gain the reputation of being concerned about the work you produce. You can, however, let the customer know that you have not done "so and so" or used a particular product yet and would be willing to try it, with the understanding (depending on your confidence level) that it may or may not come out the way it is expected. There are some customers out there who are willing to let you practice or try a technique on their quilts - with some consideration on the pricing. The best advice we can give you when you do this is to be fair to the customer. They trusted you with their quilt to practice on, and you should be fairly compensated for your services, but not at the same rate you would charge someone had you been familiar or comfortable with the technique.

Despite your best efforts, you may encounter a customer who absolutely insists that they want their project quilted in such a way that does not depict your best quilting or is against your advice. At some point, you may see this quilt in an exhibition or show with your name on it. Unfortunately, this does happen. Others will view your work as just that - "your work", not considering that the customer insisted on the quilting being done a certain way or a particular color thread that is unflattering to everyone but the customer. It is very easy for the customer to place blame on you. People who view the quilt obviously are not privy to the conversation between piecer and quilter, and only see the end result.

When you work with a quilt shop for pick up and drop off of the customer quilts, you should send the customer an e-mail when you pick up the quilt from the shop. This lets the customer know that the quilt is now in your possession. You can take the opportunity to re-affirm any information contained in the work order. Linda also sends an e-mail to let the customer know when their quilt has been loaded onto the machine, so they know they can expect the quilt to be ready within a few days.

Customers appreciate knowing ahead of time when their quilt might be completed. Many customers will ask for your "turnaround time". For the most part, they are happy when you are able to give them a ballpark figure.

As an example: You have 30 quilts waiting to be quilted. 25 are lap size easy pantographs and 5 are customs. You will do one lap size per day and each of the 5 customs will take 2 days each. You are only quilting 5   days per week. For this example, your turnaround time is approximately 6 weeks.

BE HONEST with your customers. If an accident happens, tell the customer. Don't try to hide it or cover it up. You are more likely to be forgiven by being honest up front. No one is immune from accidents.

If you make a mistake - make it right by the customer. Do not ignore the problem. Each mistake (and hopefully there won't be many) needs to be handled on an individual basis in that each incident will have its own set of unique variables.

WORKING WITH SUB-CONTRACTORS

You may wish to extend your long arm quilting business by offering additional services such as bindings, hanging sleeves and/or embellishments. You can either perform these services yourself (remember - these services take additional TIME) or you can seek out other quilters who enjoy doing binding and handwork.

Before you agree to use these quilters in your business, you should see samples of their work. Is the work up to your standards? Will they guarantee their work? Do they have the same work ethics as you do? Will that binding hold up to judging standards in a quilt show? How will they handle a customer complaint? Will they work with you as a team player (securing referrals, handing out brochures, etc)?

More than likely the quilters you choose to work with will be friends. There may come a time when you must make a business decision which can effect a friendship. For example - is the customer unsatisfied with the binding on the quilt? Speaking with the subcontractor is your responsibility because you, in essence, "hired" her to do the work on your behalf. Will this jeopardize your friendship?

When working with a sub-contractor in your long arm business here are some things to consider and discuss so there are no misunderstandings:

- How will the sub-contractor be paid? Don't forget to check with your accountant to determine the sub-contractor status.

- Who is responsible if a customer is unsatisfied with the work?

- Are you (as the owner) retaining any percentage or referral fee?

- Will you offer the sub-contractor a discount on quilting his/her personal quilts?

- Who provides the supplies for the sub-contractors, such as the thread?

- Will the sub-contractor work with you as a team player?

- Will the sub-contractor work according to the schedule you set?

- How will the sub-contractor deal with critiques?

- Is the sub-contractor a "slap 'em on, get 'em done, give me the money" type, or is she very conscientious of her work? It is vital that you know the answer to this question before you hire the person.

It is very important to communicate with your sub-contractors. Let them know when you need the quilts returned. If there is a problem with a particular quilt - let them know ahead of time.

Linda works closely with her local quilt shop and has three sub-contractors who work with her. She keeps both the quilt shop and the sub-contractors advised on the number of quilts waiting to be done and also how many of those quilts will need binding services.

DETERMINING YOUR NICHE

There are some long arm quilters who will only do custom work, which is defined as different shapes or motifs placed throughout the quilt, and there are some long arm quilters who will only do pantographs, or repeating patterns which link together.

How do you determine your niche? Research what type of quilting the other long arm businesses in your area are doing. Pay attention to the quilts displayed at quilt guild meetings' Show & Tell where members hold up their work for everyone to admire. What do you like to do? As your business progresses, you will be able to gauge the type of quilts that come into your studio, which will eventually determine your niche.

Keep in mind the pricing differences between custom quilting and pantographs. It might take you five lap size meander quilts to equal the dollar amount you would earn on one custom quilt.

PRICING

Once again, researching the prices in your geographical area will give you the best indication of what is the best pricing structure for you. Most long arm quilters will use "per square inch" method since this is the method that customers best understand.

You should have a set minimum charge. This can run anywhere from $35.00 to as much as $65.00. When setting the minimum charge, you can assume that it will only apply to small lap size quilts, baby quilts or small wall hangings. The amount charged takes into consideration the time it takes to load and unload the quilt.

Prices for large meandering begin at $0.01 per square inch or psi, though we have seen them start at $0.015 per square inch. Easy pantographs can also begin at $0.01 psi. Custom quilting begins around $0.02 psi. Depending on the quilter, this may or may not include "stitch in the ditch," where the quilting follows along the seam lines. Heirloom quilting (which includes trapunto work) can begin at $0.05 per square inch.

Pricing by the square inch is calculated by multiplying the length of the quilt top by the width of the quilt top. Next, multiply the square inches by your price (such as $.01). Here is an example: If a quilt top measures 90" by 108", it has 9,720 square inches (90 x 108). Multiply this by $.01, and price for your services becomes $97.20.

MAINTAINING YOUR CALENDAR/WAIT LIST

Longarmers use several different methods to manage their wait list and work log. There are computer software programs specific to the long arm quilting business (see our Resource section for more information). Each of the long arm software programs has work log/waiting list capabilities.

Establishing Your Niche (Linda's story)

I purchased my machine in 2004 with the intention of quilting 2-3 custom quilts each week to yield a weekly income of around $500-$700.

As the quilts began coming in, customers were not asking for the custom quilting, but rather the "get 'em done" pantos or meanders. As I started observing the type of quilts that were coming in, I could see that they fell into the "quick and easy" category. Although I was frustrated at first because this was not the type of quilting I had envisioned for my business, I realized that in my area, this is the type of quilting that is popular. I began searching out and investing in "themed" and interesting pantos.

My business is 97% pantos ("bread and butter quilting") and I always have a waiting list. My customer base is consistent and regular. My long arm business makes enough money for me to pay for 1-2 cruises per year for my family as well as our trips to the various shows, fabric, threads and anything else I would like. Will I get rich? Probably not. Am I happy? Absolutely.

You need to decide on several things as you begin taking in quilts. First, how many days and hours per week are you willing or available to work? Then, how much money are you looking to make per week or per month?

Linda uses a calendar that shows a full month. She indicates the days she is teaching, traveling or has other things to do. Linda knows approximately how long it takes to do a $0.0125 psi pantograph on a queen size quilt. An hour is allotted for loading and unloading the quilt as well as cleaning and oiling the machine, and then 2 hours to quilt the quilt. If Linda sticks to her start time of 9:00am, she will be done by 12 noon, and then have the afternoon free.

STORAGE

It is most important that your customer's quilts be given the utmost care while in your custody.

Linda suggests a 24"x24" clear plastic zipper bag which is available through Uline (see Resources). As the quilts come in to the studio, they are documented; the person who referred the customer is acknowledged or thanked (if appropriate) and inserted into the bag. Everything that belongs with that quilt stays with that quilt.

The clear zipper bags are then placed into a metal cabinet to await their turn.

PROMOS

Some longarmers, especially those who are just starting out, offer promotions or giveaways in order to build a customer base.

When you start to think about what type of giveaway would be appropriate, here is some "food for thought"... when

quilters go to classes, what do they take? Wouldn't it be nice if they all took plastic travel mugs, water bottles and/or a small insulated lunch sack imprinted with your name and logo?

Promotional items are included in your "advertising" budget for tax purposes.

In December, Linda sends out a "Happy Holiday" letter. At the bottom of the letter is a coupon for $10 off the quilting fee for quilts delivered between January and March (a typical slow time) with the return of the holiday letter. The binding girls also participate and offer $10 off of the binding price.

DONATIONS

At some point in time you will be confronted with at least one request for you to donate your services to quilt a quilt for a charitable group or a guild raffle quilt. Here are some thoughts to consider on the subject:

- Is it a charity that you support?

- Could your donating your service lead to paid jobs?

- Will this end up being a yearly donation or is it a one-shot deal?

- Could this lead to situations where you do something for one group, and must do for others?

- Will your donation be acknowledged?
- If there are several longarmers in your area, will this create an uncomfortable situation between the other longarmers and the one chosen?
- Are you expected to donate the batting, binding and hanging sleeve as well?

You might also be approached by guild people or show personnel to donate a gift certificate for a free quilting or a discounted quilting. If you decide to participate, you should be prepared to receive solicitations from others.

You may consider setting a limit on how many pro bono quilts you will do in a year. Once people are aware of this, they will get their requests in early enough that you will be able to plan them into your schedule. When you do these pro bono projects, be sure to get a receipt from the recipients verifying the value of your in-kind contribution so you can include it in your tax write-offs for the year.

RUSH CHARGES

Some quilters offer their customers the opportunity to have their quilt done on a "rush" basis. You need to decide whether it is fair to customers who have been patiently waiting their turn to be "bumped" back by someone who is willing to pay a rush charge. If you plan your schedule so you leave one day per week open for "rush" quilts, those who are waiting will still have their quilts returned on the promised date. If you do not use your "rush" date that week, you can use it as a "free" day for yourself or start on the next week's quilts.

Check the internet or advertisements for other long arm quilters in your area - what are they charging for rush orders? In the area where we live (Central New Jersey) the rush charge is 25% of the quilting charge with a $25 minimum. A rush binding charge is billed separately at the same rate.

WORK ORDER

We have included a sample long arm Work Order in the "Forms" section of this book. Please feel free to use it as a reference to create a form that fits your particular business needs.

Linda will also use the Electric Quilt computer program to print out a quilt similar to the quilt that she will be quilting in black and white outline form (no color, just the lines). She will use this to sketch out her ideas for quilting designs. She can then offer the customer several options to choose among for their quilting.

You might want to research the cost for having your work order printed with two or three carbon-less parts: one part stays with the quilt and one part is given to the customer.

PREPARATION INSTRUCTIONS

It is very important to provide your customers with instructions as to how you would like them to prepare their quilt for you. In our "Forms" section, Linda has shared a two page instruction sheet which not only provides instructions for the preparation of quilts, but also an explanation for each request. She uses this form as an opportunity to educate her customer base.

COLLECTIONS

While you do not like to think about it, there may come a time when a customer fails to pick up and pay for his or her quilt. You need to have a policy in effect, and make your customers aware of that policy, that will cover you in case such a situation arises.

Some longarmers reserve the right to donate the quilt to charity if it is not picked up or paid for within a certain number of days - this policy is clearly stated on their work order.

Some customers may have simply forgotten that their quilt was ready. A follow up phone call may be all you need to jog their memory. Be sure to note the date, time and to whom you spoke (ASK the name of the person you speak to). Some customers may have run into a financial bind and are embarrassed to tell you. If this is the case, you could offer to take payments.

If you do mail order work, we would certainly recommend that you get your payment up front before shipping the quilt out. (Ask how we know this!) Your other alternative is to get the customer's credit card number (if you accept credit cards) – see Resources for some credit card processors. You can offer an option to keep the customer's credit card number on file in a secure location so that you can automatically charge the card upon completion of the quilt.

In the unlikely event that you cannot secure payment by any of the above suggestions, you may need to file a complaint in Small Claims Court. You do not need the services of an attorney for this purpose. Check with your county court house for the appropriate forms and fees. Many court systems have their forms and instructions online.

You do NOT need to write a book on your complaint - be short and precise. In many cases the small claims court will have you attend a mediation session which is conducted by a law clerk to see if the matter can be settled prior to taking up judicial time. There is a fee for filing the complaint and you may ask that the defendant reimburse you for this as part of any settlement or judgment.

Winning a judgment does NOT guarantee collection. Once you secure a judgment, you need to collect on that judgment. This can run into even more money (which you may or may not be able to include in the judgment amount). In any event, the judgment is on the docket against the debtor and could eventually show up on a credit report.

QUILTING FOR A FELLOW PROFESSIONAL or FAMILY MEMBER

Here are some considerations for you to ponder and make a decision that's right for you and your individual business:

Will you offer a discount to a few selected local quilt teachers? The teacher might be willing to distribute coupons to his/her students in the classroom to have their class projects quilted by you for a discount.

Will you offer a discount to a pattern designer? More often than not, they will place an acknowledgement of your quilting services on their pattern - some will even provide your contact information.

Quilting for your family is sometimes difficult. They must respect the fact that you are in business to make money. Being up front with them - and perhaps providing an estimate - will avoid a potentially embarrassing and maybe even confrontational situation. If the family member knows that they are being charged ahead of time (and perhaps include a "family discount" on the invoice so they will appreciate that you acknowledged the relationship) you could happily avoid a disruption.

Chapter Six
Pattern Designing and Publishing

If you are considering offering your own line of patterns, we recommend that you purchase "Publish Your Patterns" by Nancy Restuccia (published by QuiltWoman.com). This book is a "must have" reference for the professional quilter's library.

Some quilters enter into this area unintentionally. He or she may have designed and created a quilt, entered it into a show and had inquiries from other quilters for the pattern. Simple as that. Or a teacher may offer patterns of their quilts as a way to supplement their class income, or because their students request printed patterns.

If you are planning to make a quilt specifically to offer as a pattern, you need to have an original design for your quilt. What makes your design different from what is already in the marketplace? Some say "there is nothing new under the sun," but there are new ways to look at traditional designs, innovative ways to make quilts, and different and exciting things to incorporate into quilts. Competition is tough in the printed pattern business. There are thousands of patterns on the market, but only a handful of designers will be able to earn the commitment to make a living at it. That being said, there are also new designers breaking into the market all the time. With enough commitment and enough guts, just about anyone can make it in this business.

GETTING STARTED

So, where do you begin? Most designers develop different approaches. Some will compile sketches in a sketchbook, then choose one that appeals to them as interesting and marketable. Next is doing either a graph paper sketch, or using a computer program such as Electric Quilt to map out the design, color it in (or shade it with a pencil if using graph paper), and calculate yardages.

Write a rough list of steps which will be necessary to make the project. Merry May writes out her instructions on paper, along with rough sketches of potential diagrams, then lets the instructions sit for a few days. When she goes back to her notes, she begins to make her sample, following the calculations and notes she made previously. When she finds inconsistencies, she makes note of them, and corrects them as she goes. Once the sample is completed, she does the "official" pattern writing on her computer.

Some designers will include exact diagrams of how to cut your fabric, which is a good thing if the cutting is complicated, or uses every square inch of a fat quarter, for example.

When writing your instructions, make sure you check and recheck your calculations for yardages. There is nothing worse than getting halfway through a project and discovering that you do not have enough fabric. As luck would have it, the shop where you purchased your fabric will probably no longer have it when you go back for more.

You should make your project at least twice and make notes as you go along. As you do this, you could make the project in two different colorways in order to give your customers some ideas as you make your two test projects.

Will you be quilting the quilts yourself, or will you use the services of a long arm machine quilter? You can negotiate with your quilter for a discount on his or her

fee. Will you be including the quilter's name and contact information on or in your pattern? Will this be a one-time quilting or will you send all of your work to that quilter? Will the quilter prioritize your quilts and work under time constraints?

WRITING YOUR INSTRUCTIONS

Next, you need to "bond" with your computer and write your instructions so other people can make the project just like you did. The instruction pages should be clean and concise. Be sure to include diagrams and photographs whenever possible to illustrate anything tricky or different. If you are having your quilt machine quilted by a longarm quilter, you may be able to do much of your pattern writing while your sample is being quilted.

You will also need to design an attractive pattern cover with a good photograph of the finished project, and format your supply list so it fits on a half-sheet of paper for the pattern back. This way someone who picks up your pattern will know how much fabric, as well as any other special products, they need in order to make the project. If you are not computer literate, you may be able to contact a local college or vocational school with a graphic design department, and ask them for some help.

When you are photographing your quilt for the pattern cover - a head-on, clear and crisp color shot is the best. You do not need to include Fido or Fluffy. You may or may not choose to use the services of a professional quilt photographer.

You can have the photograph printed directly onto the cover page, or you can attach an actual photo with a glue stick. It wouldn't hurt to include a photo of the quilt with an alternate colorway or fabric line. Many quilters have difficulty seeing outside the box and imagining the quilt in alternative colors/fabrics from the cover shot.

TESTING, TESTING

Next, consider sending your design and pattern instructions to a "tester". The tester could be a friend or perhaps an associate. Friends may or may not be a good choice because of the relationship. Will they be honest or will they try to not hurt your feelings? You need to be able to take constructive criticism.

When you use a pattern tester, it is important that you both agree on the arrangements ahead of time so there are no misunderstandings. How will the tester be paid, if at all? Some of the designers we interviewed provide fabric for the project for the tester, and then also provide the tester with additional fabric for a quilt of their own. Some designers will acknowledge the tester on their pattern cover as a special thank you. It is very important that you have an open line of communication with your tester so that you can get the very best feedback. Lacey June Hill of Golden Thyme Designs will host a "playdate" with her testers and provide snacks and beverages for them. In this fashion, she can observe any comments or frustrations firsthand.

PRINTING AND PACKAGING

Unless you have an industrial type printer or photocopier, you may want to consider the services of an office supply store for your printing needs. Consider the cost of the paper and printer ink as well as the wear and tear on the machine. How many sheets per minute will your printer print as opposed to the high power machines at the office supply store? They may also be able to provide you with collating and folding services.

Depending on the cost factor, you may want to consider "employing" your family members for folding and stuffing. As we discuss elsewhere in this book, you may be able to get away with dinner at a favorite restaurant as compensation. Teens might need cash, so you should be prepared to negotiate. One of the benefits of having your family members help is that this could be a bit of family time, when you can have a conversation with your kids about what is going on in their lives. You might want to consider paying by the piece, rather than by the hour, in order to encourage efficiency.

Some office supply stores offer coupons from time to time. The more you print, the bigger your discount. If you obtain a store "rewards" card, you can also get additional coupons for bigger discounts or freebies.

Some designers will print their pattern pages on colored paper which makes it more difficult to photocopy, while others will print on 8 1/2" x 14" paper or larger, again, making it more difficult to photocopy.

One advantage of printing at home would be the ability to print on demand as opposed to having perhaps several hundred patterns sitting in your studio.

Bags for your patterns should have a vent hole to get rid of the excess air in the bag. And for heaven's sake, get bags with hang holes already punched in them. There is nothing more aggravating for shop owners than buying patterns and discovering they have to hand punch the hang holes in the bags with a paper punch. See Resources for some suggestions on where to find bags.

A recent trend in packaging patterns is to use the "crystal clear" bags. Although they may enhance the colors on your pattern cover, they are not as durable as the traditional poly bags. Do a little research before committing to purchasing 1,000 or more bags, which is the usual minimum purchase.

Lacey stores her patterns at home in a plastic storage container with the patterns upright for easy inventory. Each bin has the name of the pattern affixed to the outside.

PRICING

How do you price your patterns? First you need to be cognizant of the costs involved to print your pattern.

- Price of bags
- Price for cover photograph (are you printing in color or using an actual photo glued to the cover page?)
- Price for printing
- Price for folding
- Advertising brochure and/or classified or display ads

You also should factor in the cost for making the sample and your time, so for this exercise, we'll use the following figures:

- 15 hours to design and write the pattern @ $8.00 or minimum wage
- 10 hours to make the quilt ($8.00 or minimum wage)
- $75.00 for fabric for the quilt
- $50.00 for quilting and finishing

Before you sell your first pattern, you have expended 25 hours of your time at minimum wage ($200.00) and then another $125.00 to have a finished quilt - so you have $325.00 invested. You can now add in the price for the actual production of your pattern. Are you going to Quilt Market or another wholesale trade show? Those costs are not figured into this example.

One more thing to consider is the current "going rate" for patterns. How much are comparable patterns selling for in your area? If a pattern with a color cover and one black and white page of instructions is selling for $7, but your pattern has three pages of instructions, is $7 still a fair price, both to you and the consumer? One thing you do not want to do is overprice your patterns. In the current economy overpricing is a sure-fire way to put yourself out of business quickly. Merry's view on this is to give the customer more than they expected, but no less than they need, especially when you are just getting started. This means providing a good value for the money, but with perhaps an extra color photo in the pattern. If you are providing a "bonus" of some sort (perhaps a table runner version of the larger pattern), be sure to highlight it on the front cover of the pattern, so the consumer will know they are getting something extra for their hard-earned money.

At the time we are writing this book, the price for patterns range in the vicinity of $7.00 - $14.00. Wholesalers expect to pay one-half of the retail price. Distributors expect to pay an even smaller percentage (ex. 15% off of the wholesale price). Can you sell your patterns for $2.50 each to a distributor and still make a profit?

One of the big issues in the quilting

industry today is copyright infringement. You may think that copyright infringement is a term that only applies to people or companies which copy another person's work on a large scale, but it really applies to anyone who is copying anything without the copyright holder's permission. Every time you copy a pattern to "share" with a friend, whether it is an individual pattern or something from a book, you are diminishing the income of the copyright holder. This is similar to the well-publicized issue of "sharing" music online.

Be sure to put the copyright symbol on every page of your pattern in order to protect yourself. It is not necessary to register a copyright on every pattern unless you anticipate the need to defend it.

As we have detailed throughout this chapter, it takes much more than a simple photocopy to produce original designs. The designer has a lot invested in their work, and deserves to be able to make some money as a result of their investments. If you came up with an original idea and wanted to make some money from it, wouldn't you be upset to find someone copying your pattern?

The one and only exception to the copying rule is if you are making a copy for your own personal use. This means the copy is only so you don't need to cut the original pattern sheet in order to make the project. Any other copying is an infringement.

Bottom line: Please don't cheat the designer out of their hard-earned income. We will cover this issue in more depth in our Business Issues chapter.

MARKETING

Now that your quilts are made and your pattern has been tested and written, you have some decisions to make. How do I get this pattern to the consumer??? We've included several options for you to consider which best fits into your individual business and budget.

Our publisher, QuiltWoman.com, offers an opportunity for professional designers to reach a broader audience with their patterns than they could on their own. Distributors cannot profitably purchase designs from thousands of individual designers. QuiltWoman.com carries over 300 patterns by 30+ designers, making it a great resource for new patterns for distributors. Services range from writing a pattern from scratch to taking the designer's computer files and making minimal changes. Bar codes are provided at no cost to the designer. In fact, the only time a designer is charged for anything is when they wish to purchase patterns to sell to their local shops. At QuiltWoman.com, all patterns are printed on demand. This means orders are printed as they come in and usually ship within one day. This saves all the expenses of inventory and shipping. Therefore, they can offer a higher royalty to the designers and provide fast service to their customers. They sell retail, wholesale, and to every distributor in the U.S., including catalog companies, and the largest ones in Canada. Designers may email photos of their designs to info@quiltwoman.com for feedback and more information.

You can "shop" your pattern around to the individual distributors and catalogs (see Resources for a list of distributors).

You can also pay a visit to your area quilt shops to inquire if they would like to offer your patterns at their shop. Doing a bit of legwork, or having a booth at a local quilt show will enable you to test market your designs before making the investment in a journey to Quilt Market.

Being an individual vendor at Quilt Market is a huge investment, so make sure you are prepared for the expense and the commitment to having a professional looking booth there. You may wish to inquire with one or more of the distributors (such as QuiltWoman.com) to see if you can "sponsor" a portion of their booth with displays of your quilt samples and patterns. This investment is a small portion of the cost of going to Market on your own.

Successful pattern designers may eventually be offered the opportunity to merge several patterns into a book. This is the case with Miss Rosie's Quilt Co. and Atkinson Designs, to name only two. We will cover book publishing in another section of this chapter.

Once your patterns are published, and especially if you advertise, you will begin receiving solicitations for donations for quilt shows, quilt guilds and other quilting activities. The choice to donate or even respond is up to you. What will it get you? Maybe a thank you, maybe a mention in the show program book. Eventually you will come to the conclusion that you are being asked for a lot of handouts from people who are not necessarily your customers. Some small companies will set a dollar amount on their annual donations. Once those donations have been distributed, they will turn down any other requests. It is a good idea to put in writing your policy for providing donations, and then stick with it. Otherwise you may find yourself giving away a large percentage of your profits.

PUBLISHING

There are numerous opportunities for the quilt professional within the publishing area of the quilting industry. These can be found not only in the publishing of one's own designs and patterns, but also in magazines and books.

PERIODICALS (Magazines)

Working For a Magazine

At a magazine, you will find the editor in chief (who is the person in charge of putting the entire magazine together), editors (who can be sub-divided into departments such as editing the written articles, technical aspects, advertising and photography). A managing editor keeps the magazine moving at the appropriate pace to move it through the publishing process. Each department has employees who work full time (in-house) or part time (at home).

Jean Ann Wright, (former editor of Quilt Magazine, now the editor of the National Quilting Association's Quilting Quarterly), describes her job as editor in chief as having "the ultimate responsibility for every picture and every word on every page."

In addition to these departments, you will find job opportunities in the business office. These jobs can include marketing and sales, bookkeeping, archiving, circulation, photography, layout, and customer service.

From our research, we learned that it is not mandatory that you hold any type of degree in order to work for a quilting magazine. However, a degree in journalism or English is helpful. A comprehensive knowledge of quilting is a must for the editorial staff. You should also be able to be cognizant and up to date on the various fabrics and trends within the industry.

The salary range varies greatly, depending on your geographical area, experience, the number of magazines per year, and of course, your position. A full time position (depending on your experience and background) could start at $60,000 and go upwards. Payment for freelance articles can run from $100 on up, depending on the magazine and whether or not the pattern instructions are purchased.

Working With a Magazine

The patterns and articles in each magazine come from several sources, one of which is the freelance contributor. Contributors are freelance writers, designers and photographers who submit their work to be considered for publication. Magazines can receive several dozen submissions every month from freelance designers and writers. Some magazine editors will visit various quilt shows across the country to seek out quilts to feature in their magazine.

In addition to quilt designs, you can also contribute to a magazine by writing an article. Articles can be written about a particular quilter, designer, shop, activity, historic event, technique or thought process. Before you submit your article, it is wise to "query" the editor to determine if your article fits in with the "flavor" of the magazine.

Querying simply involves sending a letter with a snapshot or two of your proposed designs, or a paragraph about the article you would like to submit. Most magazines have detailed information near the front of each issue about submissions. In addition, many magazines will now accept queries online.

Magazines usually work on a 3-6 month lead time. This means they will be working on several issues at any given time. You may have a better chance of having your work accepted if your timing coincides with one of the newer issues the publisher is working on.

Magazines will usually purchase "First Publication Rights", which means that the magazine pays you for the right to be the first to publish the photograph and/or instructions for your quilt. If you have a pattern available for the particular quilt, you may not sell it until the term of your agreement with the magazine expires. You may also negotiate with the magazine to offer kits for the quilt.

Some magazines are more advertising-based than others. This means that quilts that have been designed by fabric company designers or using fabrics from an advertiser are used more frequently than those contributed by freelance designers.

More detailed information about publishing your designs and publishing in magazines can be found in the book, "Publish Your Patterns" by Nancy Restuccia (QuiltWoman.com).

To become involved with the publishing area, you should do your best to attend Quilt Market. Quilt Market is a wholesale show geared toward the quilting industry. It is held in the fall (usually late October) in Houston, Texas, and moves around the Northern half of the country each spring (usually in mid-May). Everyone who is a serious participant in the quilting world is at Quilt Market and you will be able to meet the various publishers and editors in person. "Credentials" are required for admittance. You can view the criteria and apply for credentials at www.quilts.com.

Editors are always concerned about copyright issues. As you will read elsewhere in this book, copyright remains THE biggest issue in the quilting world. Although editors try to remain on top of what is being published in books and magazines, they also will try to rely on the honesty and integrity of the designer that the quilt or pattern they are submitting is not the design of another (with just the fabrics changed).

BOOK AUTHOR

Many, many quilters dream of one day writing a book. Unless you are continuously writing books, the income can be limited to the "life" of the book. The "life," or time frame when the book is selling well, can be anywhere from 6 months to several years.

Once you have an idea in mind, you need to search out a publisher who will advertise and publish your book. Research different publishers to determine where your book will "fit in" to their offerings. Publishers will provide you with their Submission Guidelines. Most publishers have their guidelines available online. See our Resources section for a partial list of potential publishers.

Although most Submission Guidelines generally require the same information, the format in which it is to be submitted will vary from publisher to publisher. It is very important that you follow the Guidelines completely and be as accurate as possible.

One part of the Submission Guidelines will be an Author Questionnaire. The Questionnaire will consist of your contact information and your qualifications for writing the book, such as teaching information, publications in which your work has appeared, and an autobiography. A one-page resumé is highly recommended for inclusion in your proposal.

The next part of the Submission Guidelines will be a Book Questionnaire, which requests specific information about your book. This information will include an outline of your book including table of contents, chapters, and projects. This is where you get the opportunity to "sell" your book to the publisher. You may also be asked to describe your intended audience, promotional ideas and what you envision your book to be. You will also want to point out what makes your book different from those already on the market. Some publishers may ask for a sample chapter in order to see your writing style and others may ask for a sample project. Read the Submission Guidelines carefully because you may be rejected for not following them.

Once your proposal is received at the publisher's office, it is reviewed by the Acquisitions Editor. Publishers have meetings on a regular basis in which they discuss and review each submission to determine if it will fit into their budget, and plan for the upcoming year. This may take from a month to six months from the time your submission is received to when you receive a notification from the publisher.

It is at this time that you may receive a "rejection" letter. Although you may be disappointed (and you will be), do not get discouraged. Your book may not be right for THAT publisher. You may then forward your proposal to another publisher.

You should only submit your proposal to one publisher at a time. Do not submit simultaneously to several publishers. Some potential authors will include a note with their submission asking for an answer from the publisher within a specific period of time (for example, three or four months). This enables them to submit their proposal to another publisher without waiting for an extended period of time.

If you are one of the lucky ones who receive an acceptance letter from a publisher, you will also receive a contract. All contracts are subject to negotiation and obviously you will have more negotiating leverage if you have had one or more books published, or are a well-established "celebrity" in the quilting world.

The contract will include the responsibilities and expectations of each party. It will also include an indication of whether or not you will receive an "advance," which is payment in anticipation of sales, and/or perhaps an allowance to cover photography or graphic costs. The contract will also discuss your "royalty" payments which is how authors are paid - specifically the percentage of each book sale that you will be paid as well as the frequency of the payments. An advance may be several thousand dollars, depending on the estimated sales potential of the book. For an excellent article about Royalty payments, go to http://www.ivanhoffman.com/royalties.html

The contract will contain a time line for completion of your book. You will have a deadline for when the first draft is due, and then another deadline when the final draft is due. You must be aware of and work within your time line.

You will be assigned an editor for your book. The editor's job is to guide you through the process and provide guidance with your writing process.

It is highly recommended that you review your contract with an attorney before signing it. Don't be afraid to ask your publisher questions if you do not understand something.

Your contract will provide information on how you can purchase copies of your book. Typically, authors can purchase their book from the publisher at distributor prices. You may then sell your book to local retailers at the wholesale price, earning the difference between the distributor price and the wholesale price. This could be the case if you are at a book signing hosted by a local quilt shop or bookseller. If you sell directly to consumers, such as at a quilt show, you will of course earn more from each sale. Be aware that if you are selling your books at a show, you may be required to pay for a vendor's booth, which will obviously cut into your profits. You may also be responsible for collecting and reporting sales tax depending on your location.

You need to be aware that retailers are in business to make a profit just like you are. In order to sell more books, you will need to work with them in a manner that is beneficial to both of you. Yes, you may be earning a smaller percentage per book sale if you sell at wholesale to the retailer, but in the long run the retailer is much more likely to support you in future endeavors if you help support them. They may also be paying for advertising to encourage more people to attend a book signing, setting up refreshments, and hiring extra staff to cover the additional sales.

Don't forget to purchase enough books to provide to your contributors as a gesture of appreciation for their assistance. Be sure to provide personalized autographs for them, too.

You may be asked to participate in other activities which will help in the promotion of your book, such as attending Quilt Market and assisting in the publisher's booth. This is another issue to be discussed with your publisher. Will your expenses be paid by the publisher, or are you responsible for payment of your own expenses?

SELF-PUBLISHING

Self-publishing a book is another option for you to consider. Aside from the actual printing and binding costs, you will also be responsible for your own promotional costs, editing, proofreading, obtaining an ISBN number, photography, graphics, registering your own copyright, cover design, getting a bar code, and much more.

Please see our Resources section for web sites with more information about ISBNs and bar codes. Be aware that obtaining a bar code number and ISBN is neither free nor inexpensive. You need to weigh the costs of obtaining these with the potential income from your books and patterns.

Although the income potential is much greater when you self-publish, there is far more work involved than you may initially imagine. We highly recommend doing some reading on the subject before you make any major commitments to this strategy.

Chapter Seven
Quilt Appraiser

The popular PBS show, "Antiques Roadshow" has sparked interest in becoming an appraiser. Becoming a full-fledged appraiser is not as easy as it looks, just like ice skating isn't as easy as it looks on TV.

To become an appraiser takes years of exposure to antique quilts of all ages and conditions. Many people start out as collectors of antique textiles, and eventually decide to put their hard-earned knowledge to good use.

As you begin to collect quilts, curiosity compels you to learn how to do research on the patterns, colors, fabrics, fads, and the environment of the quilt maker. This includes the historic events which surrounded her or him, her economic status, where she lived at the time she made the quilt, and many other intangible influences. Historic items do not appear from within a bubble; they are directly related to their surroundings. Becoming a quilt "detective" who can accurately identify the unspoken, unwritten characteristics of an antique quilt means, as one historian put it, "You have to flap a lot of quilts."

There is a well organized program which is run by the American Quilters' Society in Paducah, Kentucky whose goal is to award certification to people who are qualified to provide appraisals to clients for insurance, fair market value, or donation purposes. Those who achieve certification have invested a lot of time, effort and money in studying quilts, both antique and new, and have proven their knowledge before a panel of other appraisers.

According to the AQS Appraiser Certification Program application, the Requirements for Certification are as follows:

- All certified appraisers must be able to demonstrate extensive knowledge about the process and procedures used in their appraisal profession and:
- Understand the difference between insurance value, fair market value, and donation value.
- Understand the differences between insurance appraisal, written documentation, and research.
- Establish a circa date for any quilt.
- Determine fabric fiber content.
- Recognize and describe construction and finishing techniques.
- Determine the quality of construction and the quality of quilting and the effect on value.
- Determine the condition of a quilt and recognize alteration, conservation, or restoration.
- Identify patterns.
- Recognize major historical trends and influences in quilt making.
- Determine the effect of visual impact on the value of a quilt.
- Recognize and record appropriate provenance.
- Use accepted appraisal practices, procedures, and vocabulary when dealing with a client.
- Accept and support the ethical practices of the program.
- Have enough knowledge/experience to set realistic values on quilts and quilted textiles which can be substantiated in a court of law.
- Recognize personal limits of knowledge, abilities, and experience with regard to all other   appraisers and be willing to refer clients accordingly.
- Maintain professional courtesy with other appraisers.

- Purchase the official embosser; use recommended AQS appraisal form(s) that comply with Uniform Standards of Professional Appraisal Practice (USPAP; see Resources) standards

The application process requires a fee ($75 in 2008), the completed application form which is several pages long and must be typed, and copies of two appraisals you have already done. Applications must be submitted by June 1 for testing the following April.

AQS offers a number of courses in their "School of Professional Development" you may wish to take before submitting your application; however they all require a pilgrimage to Paducah, Kentucky during the annual AQS show, usually held in April. Taking the courses is neither a prerequisite nor a guarantee of certification as an appraiser.

The AQS Appraisal site has a number of links to other sites with things like a sample appraisal form, recommended books for appraisal course study, and much more.

After your application has been accepted, you must take both a written test and an oral examination during the AQS show in Paducah in April. There is a fee for the tests ($150 in 2008) in addition to the application fee.

Once you have achieved your certification, you must maintain your certification by paying a recertification fee ($100 in 2008) every three years, and prove that you are still active and learning as an appraiser.

For more information on the Appraiser Certification Program through the American Quilters' Society, visit their web site at: http://www.americanquilter.com/about_aqs/appraisal_program.php

The income potential for appraisers depends a lot on how much time you wish to dedicate to this career. By becoming a certified appraiser, you will be included on a list through the AQS which will enable the general public to find you, as well as museums and anyone else who may need to have a professional appraisal. In 2008 the "going rate" appears to be $35-40 per item for written appraisals. However, those with more experience and with good credentials can earn as much as $200 per quilt.

Keep in mind that you are not obligated to become a **certified** appraiser. With enough experience you are permitted to do appraisals on your own. The Internal Revenue Service requires appraisers to simply be a "recognized authority" in their field. As long as you have enough knowledge and experience behind you, and can substantiate the reasoning behind your professional appraisal in a court of law, you can still be an appraiser.

LEARNING MORE ABOUT QUILT HISTORY

One way to get started in learning about dating antique quilts is by joining a quilt study group. These are usually regional groups which meet periodically to study antique quilts in the attendees' collections. They often will suggest bringing quilts from a certain time period so everyone can compare a wide range of quilts. The groups usually keep in touch through e-mail lists. To see if you can find a group in your area, you may wish to make use of a list which is available through the Quilt History portal. Visit http://quilthistory.com/study/ for direct links to quilt study groups throughout the U.S. and beyond. They also have an online discussion group you may join, which provides almost daily conversations on topics related to quilt history.

The Quilt History site was established and is maintained by Kris Driessen. The site has taken on a life of its own over the years. It includes resource information for a wide range of topics related to quilt history. The main web site is at: http://quilthistory.com

Another great resource is the American Quilt Study Group, an organization whose mission is to research and document quilts and quilt-related topics with an emphasis on the highest quality standards and accuracy. "We stimulate, nurture, and affirm engagement in quilt studies and provide opportunities for its dissemination."

AQSG holds an annual Seminar (usually in October) where original research papers are presented and subsequently published in their annual journal "Uncoverings." These journals are a rich resource of information on a wide variety of topics relating to quilts and quilt makers. Membership in AQSG includes their quarterly publication "Blanket Statements," which offers news about researchers' ongoing projects, brief articles on quilt history and related topics, and much more.

If you are at all interested in quilt history, whether it is through appraisals, restoration, or any other means, the American Quilt Study Group is an important resource. We hope you will make good use of it, and at the same time consider making a contribution by way of sharing your own original research with them. For more information about AQSG, visit their web site at http://americanquiltstudygroup.org/

Another valuable web site is through the Alliance for American Quilts, where you can access their Quilt Index and research quilts by pattern name, quilt maker, location, time period and much more. The web site for the Quilt Index is: http://www.centerforthequilt.org/quiltindex.html

A second huge database is available through the International Quilt Study Center & Museum at: http://www.quiltstudy.org Once you reach their home page, look for the link to "Collections Database." From here you can research thousands of quilts, both new and old. An exciting new feature is their Explorer Timeline, where you can view objects and events chronologically. It is located at: http://explorer.quiltstudy.org/timeline.html Click on the individual images for more information.

Another way to gain experience in identifying and learning about values is by attending public auctions which include quilts and other textiles. Attending auctions in person is one of the best ways to learn quickly, because you have the benefit of being able to examine the quilts up close. This enables you to see any restorations, and also begin to learn about imported quilts which are being passed off as "antique." For example, if you find a quilt with polyester batting, it could not have been completed before the mid-to-late 1950s.

Also be aware that prices will vary depending on what part of the country the quilt is in. For example, a signature quilt which includes the names of numerous people from various towns in Vermont will bring a much higher price if it is offered for sale in Vermont than it will if it is offered in Delaware.

Of course you can research quilts (both old and new) online through web sites such as eBay®. However, it is not the same as seeing the quilts in person and being able to examine them closely. This is a good way to keep up with values on the open market so you can keep tabs on what is popular at the present time, and see how and why the values can fluctuate so widely.

You can also do a lot of research simply by going to quilt shows which include antique quilt dealers. Quilt dealers are very knowledgeable people who are usually willing to share some of what they have learned with you. Be sure to explain that you are considering becoming a certified appraiser, and are trying to learn about dating quilts and how to set a value on them. At the same time, try to be courteous and not take a lot of the dealer's time during the show, especially if their booth is crowded. You could ask for the dealer's business card and either talk to them on the phone, or contact them by e-mail at a more convenient time.

Becoming an appraiser is not something you can accomplish overnight, nor by taking one or two courses of study. It is done through a lot of hard work and constant research. Even after gaining your certification, you must continue to research values and trends. In other words, there is a significant investment of your time in order to keep up with the current values and ongoing historical research.

You will also want to monitor new quilt history books as they become available. There are a number of books featuring quilts from different areas of the U.S. and beyond. Some are better than others, but they all have good photos and can help you learn about colors, patterns, and history in general.

Other books which may be helpful are any books written by Barbara Brackman. Please see our Resources section for a number of books written by this master quilt historian. Better yet, go to her web site and do some exploration of your own at: http://www.barbarabrackman.com

EVALUATING CONTEMPORARY QUILTS

Keep in mind that appraisers also must be able to set a monetary value on new quilts. This involves a whole different set of knowledge. You will need to keep up on current trends in quilt making and quilt makers.

Today nearly everyone who makes quilts may be researched on the internet in some capacity or other, which may help you in researching the quilt maker. Some quilt makers have made names for themselves, some have a history of being able to command large sums for their work, and many are simply making quilts for the sheer pleasure of it. These are just a few of the many factors that can influence the value of a quilt.

OTHER ISSUES

Today, most museums have more quilts than they know what to do with, and because of limited funding they struggle to care for these fragile textiles. It can be a bit tricky to convince a quilt's owner that their family quilt is not of the highest caliber for museums to consider acquiring. However, sometimes museums can still make good use of donated quilts by selling them to raise funds to care for the quilts they already have. Be sure to

explain this to anyone who is considering donating their quilt to a museum.

Sometimes family history will tell you a vastly different story from what your experience as an appraiser will tell you. You must be able to gently convey what the quilt is telling you without being confrontational. This is where some of the books you will collect along the way will be of assistance, such as Elaine Jahnke Trestain's "Dating Fabrics: A Color Guide 1800 - 1960" and her second book which covers fabrics from 1950 - 2000. Both books are available through the American Quilter's Society web site (see Resources).

In any case, the quilt is important enough to the family for them to entrust the quilt's evaluation to you. Sometimes the family will think the quilt is worth far more than your assessment reveals. You must be able to assure them that, while the quilt is priceless to them, it is only worth what it will bring on the open market.

SUMMARY

It will take a lot of studying to become knowledgeable enough to become a quilt appraiser, but most appraisers will tell you that it is well worth the time, effort and money they invest in this rewarding career. We explained a little about the amount of knowledge you need, which of course will take at least a couple of years to acquire up front, and take a continuing effort to stay on top of. The monetary investment will involve tracking down the books you will need to study, taking as many courses as you can afford, the application and testing fees, and the journey to Paducah for the examinations. Even if you choose not to become certified, you must still be able to prove that you are knowledgeable enough to back up your appraisal in a court of law.

Experienced appraisers will tell you, however, that they get to see and touch quilts that no one else may ever see besides the quilt's owner. Some of the quilts will be ordinary but well loved, and others will be of museum quality. Regardless of why the quilt is being appraised, you have an important responsibility to educate the quilt's owner about how to care for their quilt.

Chapter Eight

Restoration

If you begin to collect antique quilts, you will eventually come across one that you wish to add to your collection, but it has "issues." These can include such things as simply being dusty, to being too dirty to bring into your home, to major condition problems.

All of these issues will lead you into learning more about how to care for your quilts, both old and new. Fortunately there are a number of web sites that provide detailed information about quilt care, including the Quilt History site which is run by Kris Driessen. Kris has spent many years gathering and sharing information about quilt care, quilt restoration, quilt history (including some volatile topics with major differences in opinion), and many other subjects. When she finds another web site with more detailed information than she can easily provide, she gives you links to these other sites.

There are several DVDs available about restoration work, and there is also an annual gathering of people who do restorations. Please see our Resources section for information on these. There have been a number of papers presented through the American Quilt Study Group over the years on restoration work as well.

If you wish to speak to true working experts on the topic, the Daughters of the American Revolution Museum in Washington, DC is a good place to take your more advanced questions, once you have gained some working knowledge on the subject. The DAR Museum has an extensive collection of quilts and other textiles. They also have monthly programs, many of which focus on their textile collection. Contact the DAR to ask about their educational programs.

One of the difficulties of doing restoration work is finding replacement fabrics that are of the same vintage as the quilt. Some restorers find these fabrics by going to yard sales; others network with fellow restorers for sources. Those who are just beginning to do restoration work may need to work with dealers who specialize in selling vintage quilts and vintage fabrics.

The first rule in restoration work is to "do no further harm" to the quilt. This means you should always leave the original fabrics as they are, rather than removing and disposing of them. You may cover the disintegrating fabric by appliquéing a piece of vintage fabric on top of the original layer, and then hand quilting over the stitches on the top layer of the quilt to mimic the original quilting stitches.

Another option is to thread baste a piece of "illusion" netting in a neutral color over the disintegrating fabric. This stabilizes what is already there and enables the client to still see the original fabric through the netting.

Documentation is another important aspect of doing restoration work. Take photos of the quilt "before" and "after" the work is done, and also write a description of what was done and where.

If a client insists on having you "wet clean" or wash their quilt, try to explain the process to them, and why wet cleaning of a fragile antique textile should always be a last resort. Try to offer some alternative methods before committing to wet cleaning. Wet cleaning weakens the fragile fibers, sometimes causing the quilt to deteriorate more quickly than if it were left in its original condition.

Charging for doing restoration work is something you need to determine for yourself. Clients should certainly be expected to reimburse you for the cost of any vintage fabrics, and obviously you will also need to include an hourly fee for your services. As you gain more experience you should also gain more clients through word of mouth, and you therefore may give yourself a raise periodically.

One of the most difficult aspects of doing restoration work is in providing the client with an estimate of the cost. You never know until you begin working on an antique quilt just how long it will take you to do the job. You may wish to tell the client that you will contact them when your fee reaches a certain dollar amount. They can then tell you to either stop, or continue until you reach another plateau. It is a good idea to collect a deposit to cover initial expenses, and then periodically ask for more money as you proceed with the job. Whatever you do, keep in touch with the client on a regular basis with updates on the progress you are making.

You will also want to have a written contract with the estimated time needed for the job, estimated cost of vintage fabrics, approximate number of hours you may need to complete the project, and any other details you decide are important. Please see our Forms section for a sample restoration contract.

Chapter Nine
Working with a Fabric Company

There are many different avenues to venture down when working with a fabric company, the most obvious being a fabric designer. There are the administrative positions such as the marketing director and art director, as well as sales positions. There are in-house employees as well as freelance employees.

You are not required to be a quilter to work for a fabric company, although a degree in textiles, marketing, business and/ or art might enhance your ability to be hired. Experience with quilting can certainly be helpful.

Our research tells us that jobs within a fabric company do not open up frequently.

Besides the coveted designer position, there are also the secretarial, office clerk, controller, web master, sales and other administrative jobs. There can also be in-house studio designers, CAD system operator, and stylist in addition to the marketing and sales force.

Salary ranges fluctuate depending on whether you are in-house or freelance, full time or part time. Just as an example, an experienced art director can earn up to $125,000 per year. Many companies offer the usual benefits of 401K, health insurance, vacation and sick pay. If your position dictates, you may also be able to attend Quilt Market.

DESIGNING FABRIC

Fabric designers can work either in-house or freelance. They work on a lead time of one year to six months.

In some cases a fabric designer is someone who has made a name for themselves in the quilting world. Fabric companies will contract with them to either design the fabrics, or approve fabrics which have been designed in-house. Some designers are known for reproducing vintage fabric designs whose copyrights have been released.

Freelance designers need an up to date computer with graphics programs such as Illustrator® and Photoshop®, both available from Adobe®.

Some designers begin with a watercolor "sketch," and then send it to the company, whose art department has someone who figures out the repeat, colors needed for printing, and other details.

Fabric lines are generally available for approximately six months. When the line has run its course, it is not reprinted unless the particular fabric is classified as a "staple" line (which means it can be used over and over again, perhaps even in conjunction with other fabric lines), or is in high demand.

Some companies will pay their fabric designers a "designer's fee" on a "per design" basis, for example $500.00. The fabric designer will also then receive a royalty of perhaps 10¢ per yard, which is paid quarterly. Other companies may pay a percentage of the sales, or a certain amount per yards printed or sold. Obviously the wider your name recognition, the more leverage you will have in negotiating a rate of pay. Well-known fabric designers are usually expected to also design a quilt using fabrics from their collection, which of course helps to sell more of the fabric. Unless they are working for the fabric company in another capacity, most fabric designers do not receive a salary.

Some companies will allow the designer to have a lot of input on the finished product, while other companies allow less input. It will all depend on the company that you work for. Being over demanding or too controlling will certainly not work in your favor. You must also be able to produce on tight deadlines, which means often working under pressure.

One of our sources pointed out that, unless you have something really new and different to offer, your chances of being successful as a fabric designer are slim.

DESIGNING & MAKING QUILT SAMPLES

Quilts need to be designed and made from the fabrics for marketing purposes. The fabric designer may prefer to design and make his or her quilt from their line, or they may hire an outside source.

If an outside source is hired, then the rate of pay needs to be negotiated depending on the complexity of the design, size of the quilt and who will own the quilt after the fabric has run its course. In 2008 the general rate is from $250 to $500 per quilt, again depending on the complexity and size of the quilt.

Any expenses involved in making the quilt such as long arm quilting or shipping are usually paid by the fabric company in addition to your fee for designing and making the quilt.

Many people who design quilts for fabric companies begin the designing process several months before the actual fabric arrives from the manufacturer by using computer programs such as Electric Quilt. They import the artwork or scans of each fabric into the program, and then design the quilt using the "virtual" fabrics. The proposed design, or in some cases, several options, are sent to the fabric company who then selects which design they want to use for promotional patterns, and any designs they want to simply show off how the fabric could be used.

If the fabric company wants to use one of the quilt designs as a promotional pattern, the designer must write a pattern, test it, and then format it for printing purposes. These patterns are often condensed down to one or two sides of a sheet of paper, so being concise is important. The designer sends the pattern to the fabric manufacturer for final proofing and approval. The fabric manufacturer then sends the original to a printer for mass-production of the pattern, which is then shown by fabric sales reps to shop owners, and often offered to them as a bonus for ordering the fabric. Pattern designers are usually paid a flat rate of $75 to $100 per pattern.

There is usually a very brief turn-around time for producing a quilted sample once the fabric comes in. In many cases the fabric company wants the finished sample within about two weeks. This of course means that the quilt maker must drop everything in order to meet the deadline. Many designers have a network of people they can call on to help them meet these tight deadlines.

Quilt designers may also find some additional income by submitting their quilt designs to magazines for publication. You are only paid once to make the quilt, though. If the fabric company pays you to make a quilt, then the magazine will not pay an additional fee to use your quilt in their magazine. Some magazines will pay a bonus to a designer whose quilt appears on their front cover, however. The quilt designer should negotiate with the fabric company over who is responsible for submitting the quilt to the magazine: the fabric company, or the individual designer.

Occasionally a magazine may choose a quilt design themselves and then want the quilt to be made with a particular fabric collection. The magazine contacts the fabric company, who provides the fabrics to the quilt maker. The quilt maker will eventually take ownership of the quilt, as a courtesy from the fabric company.

MARKETING THE FABRIC

A fabric company can produce thousands of yards of fabric for any one fabric line, but it does them no good if it is sitting in their warehouse. This is where the sales and marketing departments come into play.

Most fabric companies employ people who specialize in marketing, and they have the experience and knowledge to instinctively know how and where to market the fabric. For example, marketing directors will target certain magazines to run display ads for certain lines of fabric. They also provide samples to sales reps who show the fabric to buyers from quilt shops, chain stores, and other retail outlets.

Many people can make a living from being fabric sales representatives or reps. Some salesmen only represent one large company; others rep for several medium to small-sized companies. Income is totally dependent on how much fabric they sell to shop owners because they work on commission.

Fabric reps travel throughout a particular area called a "territory," making appointments for the shop owners to look at the newest fabrics from each company. As the reps gain more experience, they know which shops prefer to buy certain types of fabrics. For example, some shops will specialize in carrying batiks, while others go for more traditional looking fabrics.

One of the drawbacks to being a fabric rep is the transportation costs. This not only includes gas, but putting a great number of miles on your vehicle. Of course this will lead to the need to purchase a dependable new vehicle every few years.

Another potential pitfall is when a shop has ordered too much fabric and cannot pay for it in a timely manner. The fabric rep will sometimes get involved here because if the fabric company isn't paid, then the rep does not get their commission.

Chapter Ten
Professional Exhibitor

This may be a category that is limited to a small group; however, we thought that because there is potential for income we should include it. The potential income can range from $50 to $100,000 per event. However, be aware that this is not a consistent source of income for most people. The benefit of being an award winner is in the recognition and potential for income from other sources which may arise as a result of being an award winner.

The professional quilt show entrant is someone who knows their work is of high quality, and who enters their work into shows with cash and/or merchandise awards. Some of the bigger shows may include Purchase Awards, which means the sponsor becomes the new owner of your quilt. While it is an honor to have your quilt win a purchase award, it also means you will only ever see this piece by visiting a museum or by appointment, such as in the case of a private company. Some winners of purchase awards have turned them down because the quilt makers have invested too much of themselves in the piece and don't want to give it up.

Quilts that consistently win awards at different shows around the country can generate name recognition for you, which in turn can lead to other money-making opportunities in the quilting industry. For example, your winning quilt could generate other income for you by way of teaching opportunities, judging opportunities, designing opportunities, commission pieces for corporations, or for various publications.

In order to have your work accepted into a show, here are some things for you to consider:

First you need to find a show (see the Resource section for the websites of some of the larger shows). Shows are often advertised or listed in various quilt magazines. Many of the larger shows will also offer their entry forms and instructions online. Some shows also include entry forms in their program books sent to past exhibitors and class participants. If there is a show you would like to enter and you are not on their mailing list and they do not have online forms, contact the show manager who is listed in the advertisement and ask him or her to provide you with the forms. Please refer to our resource section for contact information on some of the larger shows. Also be aware that sometimes the show management will require a small fee (maybe $3) to cover their postage and printing expenses.

Once the forms arrive, it is important to read them CAREFULLY. The categories are not the same in every show. Be sure that your quilt qualifies and is entered in the correct category. If your quilt was quilted by a machine quilter, please remember to give the quilter credit. Each show has its own entry criteria, so you may be able to enter a certain category in one show, and a different category in another show. We cannot stress enough for you to read the entire entry form carefully.

Mark all of the dates for deadlines on your calendar. Most shows are very strict when it comes to following deadlines.

Many of the larger shows are juried. This process insures that there will be quality quilts for the show attendees to view. The jurying process means that entrants are expected to submit photos of the quilts they wish to enter in the show, which are then viewed by a panel of people who are chosen by the show management. The panel's job is to find the best work

which reflects the theme of the show. Be aware that panel members may not necessarily be quilters; they may be artists, museum curators, or even decorators. Juried shows usually develop when there are many more entries than space available for display in the show's venue.

If the show you have chosen to enter is juried, then there will be additional instructions for you to follow. In the past, most juried shows required slides to be submitted along with the entry form and fee. The mere inconvenience of securing good quality slides have caused many people to not even attempt to enter. Today, electronic submissions are becoming more and more acceptable.

Whether you need to submit slides or whether you submit electronically, you still need good photography. There are professional quilt photographers available to you. B.J. Titus, whose quilts win awards all over the country, used a professional photographer prior to the digital camera. Now she uses her own high quality digital camera. One of the issues which would certainly influence your decision on whether to do your own photography or whether to use a professional is TIME.

Many quilters are "down to the wire" when it comes to deadlines. You may need to adjust your work schedule in order to have your quilts completed so they can go to the photographer, and for the photographer to have the slides/photographs ready for you to submit.

The cost for 30 slides (15 full shot and 15 detail shots) currently runs at approximately $85.00. This price, of course, could be adjusted up or down depending on how many slides you actually need, how many other quilts will be photographed and your geographical area.

If your quilt is accepted into the show, you will be notified by the show management. They will usually send you more information along with your acceptance, telling you when and where to ship your quilt. Some shows have requirements and/or checklists for you to follow. You should also be aware that some shows ask for the quilts in pillowcases, others in clear plastic bags. Some specify that you may not use mailing tubes to ship your quilt(s). Please read and follow all shipping requirements. At some shows there are even preferred shippers for you to use.

There is a date range in which quilts must be received. Do not send them before or after that range. Show Management may not arrive at the host venue until a certain date. If quilts begin arriving earlier than the scheduled date, they will be put in the mail room of the venue and HOPEFULLY will make their way to the show floor.

If your quilt has been appraised (and if you are sending it to a show, it should be), a copy of the appraisal should be included with your entry form.

When we asked B.J. if there were any tips she could suggest for this chapter, she gave us the following:

- Get the best image you can afford - bad images will not get you into the show.
- The full image shot should not show your fingers, tummies or Fluffy - this is not a quilt magazine shot.
- For the detail shot, you should be able to discern the fine detail of stitching. Resist the urge to crop or enhance the image.
- Appraisals are a must if you are going to ship quilts to shows.

SHIPPING QUILTS TO AND FROM THE VENUE

The importance of photographing your quilt and having a quilt appraisal can't be stressed enough!

Have your quilt appraised by a qualified appraiser. Once you have the written appraisal in hand, make a copy and forward it to your insurance carrier so your quilt can be covered under your homeowner's policy. Depending on the coverage you have, you may need to purchase a "fine arts" rider for your policy. Be sure to ask your agent exactly what the coverage is, and what else you might be able to include under the rider. You may be surprised at what your current policy does not cover!

Once you have the insurance coverage and appraisal in hand, you are ready to ship your quilt to the show.

When packing your quilt, first of all be sure to follow all of the rules from the show entry information. If they tell you to use a pillow case, use a pillow case to pack your quilt. If they tell you not to use a pillow case, they have a reason for it, so pay attention to the instructions! One thing you must do is be sure there is a permanent label attached to the back of the quilt with your name, address and telephone number. For most judged shows, this label must then be temporarily covered by a piece of muslin which is basted over the label. This enables the quilt judges to judge your quilt without seeing anyone's names. Also in with the quilt should be the paperwork required by the show. Some shows require you to enclose a check with your paperwork to cover the cost of your return shipping. This would be attached to the other paperwork needed by the show workers. You should also enclose a separate piece of paper with your name and address, and the name and address of the place where the quilt is being shipped. This gives you an extra layer of coverage in case the box becomes damaged. Finally, make sure everything is securely wrapped inside a sturdy, clear plastic bag. Again, sometimes you hear about floods, tornadoes or other disasters, and it is possible that your package could be caught in the midst of one of them.

Take your carefully packaged box to your shipper of choice and be sure to have it insured for the amount shown on your appraisal (assuming that the appraisal was done for insurance purposes). Do not write the word "quilt" anywhere on the outside of the box!!! If the shipper asks you what you are shipping, tell them it is either a "blanket" or "bedding" in order to not attract undue attention to the true worth of what you are shipping.

Most shows will explain their policy for returning your quilt to you in with their initial paperwork, so there should be no surprises here.

COPYRIGHT or COPYWRONG?

Copyright issues can be found all over the quilt world, and exhibiting or sharing your quilts at a quilt show is not immune.

For the most part (although there are some shows which do not permit photography of certain quilts or in certain areas) when you enter your quilt in a show, you give your permission for attendees to photograph your quilt. In fact, some shows include a statement to that effect on their entry forms.

Unfortunately, there are some quilters out there who take photos of quilts they like, sketch the quilts, and even go to the extreme

of taking measurements. They then go home to make a replica of your quilt. It happens.

Do you now consider this flattery? There is the old saying that imitation is the sincerest form of flattery. Well, there is a difference between flattery and copyright violations. Please see our "Business Issues" chapter for more information about copyrights, and what you can do to help protect yourself.

PRIZE MONEY

While many professional quilters do their own quilting, a time may arise when the services of a professional quilter are used, or perhaps two professional quilters collaborate on a project.

Prior to entering into a joint venture, especially when it is the intent to create a competition quilt, all possible scenarios should be discussed and agreed upon to avoid any disruption in a friendship or business relationship. Some points to discuss - and agree upon in writing - include:

- Who pays for the materials to construct the quilt?
- Percentage of contribution of each maker?
- Who pays for the cost of the appraisal?
- Who pays for the entry fees, shipping costs, etc?
- Who will retain ownership of the quilt?
- Distribution of prize.

The most important questions here are the distribution of the award, and who gets the quilt. Money is the easiest award to divide up. Discuss ahead of time the percentage each maker will receive. When the prize is a sewing machine or a ribbon, it can become a point of contention. Who keeps the ribbon? What do you do if one person wants the sewing machine and one does not? We know of one prize that is a weekend quilter's getaway. The old adage can come into effect "money is the root of all evil" and although the topic may seem unnecessary or uncomfortable to discuss with a partner or friend in advance, it will be more uncomfortable if the failure to do so results in a loss of friendship or even a lawsuit!

SELLING YOUR QUILTS AT THE SHOW

Some shows offer you the opportunity to sell your quilt. There can be a fee involved (or not) to list your quilt as being "for sale". You can expect to pay a commission or percentage to the show sponsor. Fees can be anywhere from 10% of the sale price to 50%, so be sure to ask about this in advance! Some shows allow you to put a "for sale" sign on your quilt, but then want nothing to do with any transaction that may take place. It keeps them from being stuck in the middle in the event a dispute arises. Other shows strictly forbid you from offering to sell your quilt at their show.

We can almost guarantee that if you do sell your quilt during the show, the quilt must stay where it is until after the show closes. Picking up the quilt and then delivering it to its new owner is your responsibility. If the quilt is being shipped back to you, the new owner will have to be patient for it to reach you, and then be repacked and shipped to them. If shipping to the new owner is required, be sure to discuss the costs with the buyer before you close the deal.

If a commission is required to the show sponsor as a result of the sale, be sure to pay them promptly.

STORING YOUR QUILTS AT HOME

Quilters often come up with innovative ways of solving problems. Because of the size and nature of quilts (they can get big creases when folded), some quilters will cover a foam "noodle" (used as a toy in swimming pools) with muslin and roll their quilts around the noodle. This eliminates folds, which can detract from how a quilt looks when it is displayed. The next problem arises once you have your quilts rolled onto the noodle: where do you store this huge thing? Some quilters will lay the rolled up quilts on a bed in a spare bedroom and cover it with a clean blanket to keep dust and light away from the quilts.

Other quilters use huge cardboard tubes which are used for rolling carpet. Again they wrap muslin around the tube to keep the quilts from being discolored by the cardboard, and roll their quilts around the tube. They then have a rack where the tubes have sturdy clothes pole rods or metal pipes inserted into them, and the tubes are then hung horizontally on upright racks. This, of course, requires a whole wall you would have to sacrifice in order to allow enough space for this system.

Still other quilters fold their quilts - some use acid free paper to soften the folds - and insert them into pillow cases. The quilts are then stored in a closet, or inside a cedar lined trunk. No matter where you store your quilts, be sure they are not touching any raw wood, which can leak into the quilt and cause permanent stains. Also use common sense in storing your quilts by keeping them in climate controlled areas. We know of one person who rents a climate controlled self-storage space for her quilts!

Chapter Eleven
Judging

Quilt judging is not something that can be taken lightly. You need to be able to make a decision and stand by it. As a quilt judge, you will travel to quilt show venues to evaluate entries. You may work individually or in a team situation.

Judges should be well versed in many different techniques and be able to render an unbiased opinion, as well as communicate comments to scribes effectively. Judges must be able to put aside their personal preferences in order to be objective and fair. Another important issue is confidentiality. What happens in the judging room stays in the judging room.

Judges may earn $125.00 - $300.00 per day, although there are some who may earn more. You will be provided with round trip transportation, lodging and meals. Some shows will also hire the judge to teach at the show in addition to judging.

There are many quilters who do not understand the concept of judging. If you stand by an award winning quilt for a length of time at a quilt show, you will most likely hear at least one comment from a spectator inquiring why that particular quilt won, while the quilt that they like did not. A comment such as this stems from not understanding the judging criteria and process.

There are a good many judges who offer lectures which deal with what the judges look for - this is an excellent opportunity to educate the public.

There will be two classifications of judges that we will include in this chapter. The National Quilting Association ("NQA") certified judge and the judge who is not certified by the NQA, but has other credentials which would enable him/her to act in a judging capacity.

Show management will seek out an NQA Certified Judge, a national teacher or a notable award winner to judge their show. Smaller, local shows or county fairs might seek out their local quilt professional for judging.

At its annual show, the National Quilting Association offers a two day course entitled "Introduction to Quilt Judging". Taking this course does NOT certify you as a quilt judge, but rather provides an insight into quilt judging. This course is open to all, not just to certified judge candidates.

The National Quilting Association offers a program to certify quilt judges. The program can best be described as typical to a course of independent study. Candidates will observe a judge mentor or perhaps even several judges at numerous shows (local, regional and national). Candidates are also provided with a list of suggested reading materials to assist them in familiarizing themselves with the various styles and techniques they may encounter at quilt shows.

The program is described in detail on the NQA website: www.nqaquilts.org

During the observation or "shadowing" process, you are not permitted to interject any comments or critiques - your only purpose is to observe.

You are responsible for your own expenses incurred while attending shows in which you are observing your mentor judge.

If you enroll in the NQA Certified Judge program, you are responsible for your own travel expenses to attend at least three National Quilting Association shows, in order to volunteer as an aide in

the judging process. You must aide once before submitting the paperwork for the program, and once again before you attend a panel review. You are also responsible for payment of an enrollment fee for the Judging program.

Judges may be required to be on their feet for 8 or more hours per day. This period would include several breaks and a lunch period. Some judges will add additional fees to their contract if more hours (in a day) are required or more than a certain number of quilts will be judged.

A teaching opportunity may arise from the judging activity. In that case, you would most likely have a day or two "layover" between when the judging takes place and when the show actually starts. This allows the show management time to ensure that all the quilts are hung and the show is ready to open. Be sure your expenses are covered by the show during this layover period.

Some ethical concerns that a quilt judge might encounter include:

- Pressure from show management to make an award to a certain quilt or quilter.
- Recognizing someone's work or recognizing a friend's work. An option might be if there is more than one judge you can excuse yourself for a brief time after discussing it with the sponsors of the show. However, if you are judging alone, you must be able to distance yourself from this problem and judge with an open mind.
- The problem of feeling that there is nothing in the category that merits a blue ribbon and not awarding one. This can be brought up before judging begins so sponsors are aware that it can happen and that second place will be awarded.

- Separating yourself from the group so that you do not get pulled into agendas that others might have as to who they would like to see win.
- Always be aware that things you say could hurt someone and since you do not know who is in the room, never leave yourself open to saying something that is in poor judgment or taste. Your words must encourage and inspire in bringing out the abilities of each quilter.

If you decide that you would like to pursue judging, we suggest that you volunteer to assist on the judging floor at as many shows as possible. There are numerous opportunities to help during the judging process. A "scribe" transcribes the judge's comments to paper. This is a great way to learn the way to phrase judging comments. You may also be a "judging assistant" who will hold up quilts or perform whatever task the judge needs to make the judging move along efficiently. Try to attend shows at all levels (local, regional and national). Listen to the comments the judges make, and for that matter, do not make. Carefully observe the process. See if you are able to secure a blank copy of the evaluation form as well as the show entry form from a website. Of course, confidentiality must be maintained. The more familiar you are with the entire process, the more effective you will be as a judge.

If you are able to locate a copy of "The Judge's Task" by Patricia Morris (AQS 1993), by all means, grab it up. It is out of print, but from time to time they do become available. Patricia Morris was an extremely well respected quilt judge and basically "wrote the book" on quilt judging.

Two other very useful publications are "Judging Quilts" by Katy Christopherson and "The Challenge of Judging" - both of which are published and distributed by The Professional Quilter magazine. (See Resources.) Scott Murkin has a series of articles about quilt judging published in The Professional Quilter magazine, and Lynne Erbach has been writing a series of articles for the NQA Quilting Quarterly Magazine entitled "The Judge's Perspective". In her articles, Lynne discusses the judging process and criteria used when evaluating the techniques used in quilt making.

Chapter Twelve
Show Management

There is usually one person who has the ultimate responsibility for the operation of a Quilt Show. The Show Manager brings together all of the elements and makes it happen. The Show Manager may employ the services of one or more assistants, depending on the size of the show. The Show Manager may seek out the services of local quilters or quilt professionals to help out at the show venue during the run of the show. If you reside in the local area of a large show and would like to help, you may want to contact the Show Manager and discuss a per diem (daily) employment arrangement. Payment for per diem work depends on the size of the show and the specific job you are assigned, but the pay could be in the range of minimum wage to about $10.00 per hour.

The Show Manager should have some experience with the operation and management of a quilt show (in other words, on-the-job training). The more experience you have, the more knowledge you will have under your belt, and the more valuable you become. The Show Manager should be familiar with the needs of the vendors as well as the teachers in order to effectively communicate with them. The Show Manager should also keep themselves up to date with current trends in the quilting industry.

Opportunities in this area are limited, but nonetheless this is an avenue for income. Advertisements for Show Management opportunities can occasionally be found in the Classified Ads in various periodicals. Show Managers can work for "for profit" organizations or "not for profit" organizations.

It is difficult to determine an actual dollar amount to provide an income range. There are some Show Managers who run their own show or shows as a business for profit. The income from an arrangement such as this would depend on the actual income and expenditures from each individual show. There are some Show Managers who work as part of a larger group who could receive a fixed salary. There are also some Show Managers who receive a finite fee (such as $10,000) in addition to their expenses (phone bill, copying, hotel accommodations, travel expenses). Some may even receive a percentage of the "gate", which is defined as the show's admission fees. Show Managers for the large national level shows can work 40-50 hours per week. The one disadvantage that may arise for the not-for-profit quilt show is that the Show Managers may be unpaid volunteers and as such can change on an annual or bi-annual basis.

After you read this book and wander around your next quilt show you will be able to more closely observe the various elements involved to make this show happen. As you do so, understand that each show has its own individual qualities and offerings that make it special.

In addition to working on the current year's show, the show manager is busy at work planning shows two to three years in advance. The Show Manager wants your show experience to be both enjoyable and a learning experience.

Some of the things that a Show Manager would deal with on a regular basis would include:

Venue - Sufficient parking, dining facilities, restroom facilities, adequate and secure space to display the quilts, adequate classroom space, enough tables and chairs in the classrooms, electrical concerns for both the classroom and vendor area, telephone lines for vendor credit card machines,

security, working with the decorator who supplies the pole and drapes (for hanging the quilts, and also as backdrops in the vendor areas), and the carpeting. The Show Manager may have to make more than one personal visit to the venue.

Quilts - Arrangements for quilts to be picked up and dropped off at the venue, security, story cards, insurance, jurying process, entry form processing, creating a floor layout and hiring the judge. The Show Manager should be familiar with the full spectrum of the various categories that may be offered in which quilts can be entered in order to decide which categories would be appropriate in his or her individual show.

Classes - Offering classes for all skill levels, in a variety of subjects and techniques to appeal to all quilters.

Teachers - Seeking out and negotiating contracts with teachers to provide the required variety of classes. This includes travel arrangements, special requirements for the classroom (such as AV equipment), meals, evaluations, and assignment of classrooms. The Show Manager should be able to effectively and patiently communicate the expectations of the show to the teacher, especially when hiring a teacher who is just beginning to teach on a regional or national level. We covered Teaching in much more detail in a separate chapter.

Vendors - Seeking out and contracting with vendors who offer a variety of items, coordination of vendor booth assignments, providing vendors with easy ingress and egress to the venue, providing electrical and telephone lines for the vendors, and vendor relief (for vendors who travel alone).

Solicitation and coordination of Sponsors- Sponsors may participate by providing classroom sewing machines, or by contributing cash or other items for major prizes. Show Management should endeavor to ensure that any classroom machines are properly equipped according to the specifications for the classes in which they will be used.

Publicity - Laying out the brochure, printing and distributing flyers, postcards, bookmarks and other show advertisements, determining which magazines to advertise in at least six months in advance. Sending flyers to appropriate places for pre-show publicity. Arranging for radio or television ads.

Sounds like a lot of work, right? But wait, there's more!

After the Show Manager chooses the faculty for the show, the manager must then prepare, send out and receive the teaching contracts, along with the supply lists, photos of the class projects and teacher biographies. Once these are received, the Show Manager will then prepare and print the show catalog. The show catalogs are then addressed and mailed off to thousands of quilters all over the world.

As the quilters begin receiving their catalogs, the Show Manager's office begins receiving the class enrollments, hotel reservations (if the show handles that aspect), and questions. Accurate records of payments and class enrollments and ultimately class wait lists must be kept updated. If the show accepts credit card payments, the credit cards must be processed. Bounced checks and declined credit cards must be dealt with expeditiously. Class confirmations and necessary supply lists must be sent out to the registrants. Name tags must be printed and parking passes issued as the show's opening date approaches.

If the show has a web presence, all of the class descriptions, teacher biographies,

hotel accommodations, meals, driving directions, and other information must be entered and kept up to date.

In addition to receipt of the class registrations, the Show Management Office will start receiving quilt entries. If the show has a jury process, this must be arranged. The jury process will involve the hiring of a judge or perhaps well-known quilters to review photos of each and every quilt entry. The Show Manager will refer to their floor plan and will be aware of how many of each size quilt he or she will be able to accommodate. There needs to be a balance of the number and style of the quilts accepted. Once the jurying process is complete, acknowledgements, rejections, and shipping instructions are sent.

Before quilts and quilters arrive at the show, Show Management staff will prepare the program book. This is the book you receive when you walk through the door. The program book contains information on every quilt, exhibit, vendor and sponsor, as well as floor plans for the venue. Some shows will also order tote bags, pins and other "souvenir" items for that year's show. Award ribbons (and other prizes if appropriate) are also ordered.

The Show Manager usually will arrive at the venue approximately one week before the show begins. Quilts begin to arrive at the venue, as the Manager oversees the assembly of the hanging devices for the quilts, laying out the vendor spaces, classroom preparation and all other pre-show activities. After the boxes with the quilts are opened and sorted according to category, the judging process begins. After each category is judged, the quilts are taken to the appropriate area and hung. The list of winners needs to be prepared and inserted into the show program just before the show opens. The vendors arrive and the Show Manager or staff will ensure that each vendor is set up.

The show opens and for the duration, the Show Manager and staff are kept quite busy dealing with the many issues that can arise during a quilt show including (but certainly not limited to - and we will point out that some of the issues listed may or may not be within the Show Manager's control):

* Crowd control (there's money burning in those pocketbooks).
* Ensuring that the teachers are prepared, fed and ready to greet their students.
* Class additions and withdrawals.
* Hot dogs are cold and the Coke is warm
* Theft and/or damages.
* Last minute issues with electric in vendor or classroom areas.
* Accidents (falls and other injuries)
* Answering questions (which can be confrontational) from attendees who do not agree with the choice of the judge.
* Returning quilts which do not adhere to the entry rules (for whatever reason) as well as quilts that arrive after the time specified.
* Dealing with teacher emergencies - perhaps a teacher had a death in the family and could not make it to the show - the Show Manager needs to be able to deal with this issue fairly and expeditiously.
* Listening to people who have complaints - it is very important to maintain the good will of the show - many people just want to be heard.

The Show Manager can make a mental or even a written note of the issue or issues to be dealt with or discussed after the show, unless it is something that requires immediate attention.

Some additional frustrations that Show Management might deal with are:
* Teachers being late or incomplete in providing their information to Show Management, which delays publication of the show catalogs.
* Delays in the arrivals of teachers and/ or judge due to weather or other circumstances.
* Quilts arriving before or after the time allotment (quilts arriving before can be misplaced in the mailroom and quilts arriving late may not arrive in time to be judged) which necessitate the quilts being returned to the entrant.
* Vendors who do not comply with their contract (such as taking up more space than allotted) or who are not on time.
* Removal or covering of flyers or brochures of a competitor at the information table by other vendors.
* Teachers who use the classroom experience as an "infomercial" for their products.

We would like to point out that we interviewed several Show Managers from local, state, regional and national venues for this chapter. All of them indicated that they have (and some still do) enjoyed their experience.

Chapter Thirteen
Vending

Vendors are an important part of a quilt show. As you stroll the aisles, you will see vendors from out of state as well as local vendors. Some of the vendors are "professional" vendors who travel from show to show, state to state. For this section, we have interviewed those who vend professionally and those who vend for "exposure" purposes.

GETTING STARTED

Obviously, you will need to register your business with your state to secure a business license. You will then need to secure a sales tax ID number. This will enable you to purchase at wholesale rates. If you are going to vend in more than your home state, you will need to secure a sales tax number from each state in which you will be vending.

FINDING SHOWS

Begin by searching out your local shows. Pick up flyers for upcoming shows as you visit quilt shows. Contact the show vendor chair and request an application. You may find that there are some local shows that have relationships with vendors year after year. Don't fret...keep submitting your applications and at some point in time, you may be able to slip into a vendor space being vacated by a vendor who is retiring, moving, etc. Vendors from the prior year are usually extended an invitation to return prior to consideration of new applicants.

Many of the larger shows have vendor applications available for you to complete online. Again, you can also contact the show management and request a vendor application. Some shows are now requiring that you submit a photo of your booth along with your application.

Once you receive the application, read it over CAREFULLY. Did we say carefully? Yes, and we mean carefully. Some of the items you may discover while reading the vendor contracts:

- You may not be permitted to bring your own tables, which means you must rent them from the show sponsor or decorator.
- You must sell at retail prices. In other words, no "show special" offers - nothing may be discounted.
- You are not permitted to vend at another show within a certain radius or time period from that show.
- You cannot unload your "stuff" yourself - you must use the services of union workers for that particular venue, and they do expect to be tipped for their services.
- There may be limitations on what you can display or sell.
- Electric and/or phone lines cost extra. You will need electricity to run a cash register, and you may need a phone line to process credit card sales. See our chapter on Business Issues for more about credit card processing. If you need electricity, bring your own heavy duty extension cords in order to plug into the show's power supply, and be sure your name is on them, making them less likely to "wander off" during the show's tear-down.
- Tables must be draped to the floor; some shows require that table covers and booth "walls" (hangings) must be flame proof.
- Limits on the number of vendor badges they will issue to you.

One more thing to be aware of is the difference in the pricing and sizes of the booths which the sponsors are willing to rent to you. Local show fees can vary from only $50 for a 2-day show, up to about $150. Booth sizes can be anything from one table, up to a 10' by 12' space. Some shows include tables with the booth fee, some do not. Large shows, which can attract thousands of people, charge a much heftier fee. These begin at about $450 for the duration of the show (usually 2 or 3 days), up to $1,000 or more. Booth sizes can vary somewhat but are usually either 8' square or 10' square. Additional optional fees might include for a corner space, or a deep space (entire width of the double row). Some shows also include a stipulation that your booth must be open for sales during a Preview Night. This means after a hard day of setting up your booth (with no heat or air conditioning in the building during setup), you will be expected to be cool and calm and welcoming customers that same evening.

BOOTH SETUP

Be sure to include lots of samples! Samples sell. Think about it...what would attract you into someone's booth at a show?

You may want to mark off the size of the booth space and set up your booth at home for practice. Take photos of it and put them into a small notebook or plastic sheet for reference. This will usually enable you to set up your booth more easily. However, be aware that being in a real building with a real show can change your perspective dramatically. Your space may be on a corner, which you had not planned on when doing your practice setup. Do you open up one side of your booth, making it more open and accessible, or proceed as if there is still only one walkway where people will enter your booth?

Things to bring with you; Merry calls

this her "Office" and keeps it all in a heavy plastic tote bin with a lid. During the show, she slides it under the table where the cash register is, so she can easily pull things out, and can also keep an eye on things like her purse.

- Scotch tape & duct tape
- Pins
- Water
- Pens, note paper; perhaps a paper clip or two
- Zippered bank bag for transporting your change, daily receipts, credit card slips to be processed, and such
- Junk scissors
- Business cards plus a holder to put them in
- Bags
- Cash register, cash register tape, & heavy duty extension cord; we usually also bring a surge suppressor
- Credit card processing machine plus paper for receipts
- One or two carbon-less Sales Books, just in case of a power failure
- Battery operated calculator (just in case)

INSURANCE

With the thousands of dollars worth of quilts on display, as well as liability for the people – both working and visiting, vendors, and all of the other things that are involved in a show, you obviously need to obtain insurance. In many cases, the fee collected from the show entrants (those who are exhibiting quilts) includes a portion to help cover the cost of the insurance. The Show Manager must speak with an agent who will provide the necessary coverage, depending on the size of the show. Non-profit quilt guilds can obtain coverage through the National

Quilting Association, provided that their guild is a member of the NQA.

SECURITY

Many of us have heard horror stories about quilts being stolen from shows. A professional security staff can help to prevent such a loss, as well as keep an eye on the money being collected at Admissions, and possibly also help in the vendor area to prevent shoplifting. In addition, you will need 24-hour coverage during the show to ensure that unauthorized people do not enter the show area after hours. Smaller guild shows sometimes have members do "sleepovers" to cover this, while larger shows would need to hire an outside company. White Glove hostess volunteers can help somewhat by keeping an eye on people who may be getting too close to the quilts, but they are not trained as security guards. If something unusual happens, they need to be able to contact an authority quickly, who can then react appropriately to the situation.

BAGS

Some vendors use plastic "t-shirt" bags (such as you receive at the grocery store). Others use purchased shopping bags with a label or rubber stamp pressed onto the bag. Some bags are even "decorated" with a strip of fabric or ribbon tied to the handle. This can be nice, simple advertising - as you walk through the show, people will see a pretty bag and notice the label on it. See our Resources for sources for ordering bags.

CHARGE CARDS

It is really a necessity any more to accept credit card sales. If you vend frequently, you might want to look into an electronic credit card processing machine. Besides the cost for the equipment which you must either purchase or lease, you should be aware that this may add additional expense to your booth space by requiring a phone line and electricity. Many vendors use manual machines (also known as "knuckle crunchers") and then run the credit cards when they return home or to their hotel at night. If you are processing your sales from a hotel, be sure to check on any phone charges. Some hotels now charge you even if you dial a toll free number. We will address credit card processing in further detail in our "Business Issues" chapter.

MERCHANDISE

Please refer to our Resources section which lists some of the major distributors in the United States. Contact the credit department of each distributor to apply for credit. You can establish automatic billing for your credit card, or apply for a net 30 day payment arrangement. As you review each of the distributors' websites, you will note that some carry certain items and some do not. Each distributor has their own minimum order requirements, and they also often have minimum quantities per item. For example, you may only want three of a certain notion, but the distributor will only sell them to you in a box of six. Review and consider which distributor works best for you. Some of them process and ship more quickly than others.

If you are not a brick and mortar store, you may be imposed an additional shipping charge for delivery to a residential address. Some distributors offer free shipping for orders over a certain amount, and some will ship certain items for free. You can also arrange for the distributor to ship items to you at your destination or the show venue.

If you need a substantial amount of a certain product (pattern, template, etc), you may want to contact the manufacturer directly and negotiate a price. Distributors sometimes carry limited quantities of certain products.

If you are a teacher, you obviously want to be able to offer enough templates, patterns, etc. for each student. It may not be cost effective for you to purchase 60 of each item and then "be stuck" if students do not purchase them. You can contact the distributors and sometimes make arrangements to purchase the items on consignment.

Most distributors will provide you with a "call tag" if they send the wrong item or a damaged item. If you change your mind, however, you will most likely be responsible for a "restocking" fee as well as be responsible for the return shipping costs.

STORAGE

Linda uses plastic bins - one for patterns, one for threads, etc. When she leaves to do a lecture, she is able to grab the box which contains lecture specific items to bring with her.

DEMOS

There's no doubt about it...demos will help you sell products. A small table set up in your booth and a progression of samples will not only bring people over to see what you are doing, but in all likelihood could result in sales.

If you are offered an opportunity to present a short demo at the show, jump on the opportunity. You are usually not permitted to collect money during your demo, but you are allowed to send people to your booth to make their purchases. Make sure you have someone covering your booth while you are in the demo area who can handle the volume of sales they will suddenly be confronted with!

Don't be pushy. Not everyone who walks into your booth is going to buy something.

Greet everyone who walks in, and be welcoming, even if your sales are in a slump.

It is acceptable to do some up-selling; for instance if someone purchases a metallic thread, you could ask if they need metallic needles to go with them. If someone buys a pattern which suggests a particular ruler, ask if they also would like to purchase the ruler. You may be surprised at the difference in your sales by the end of the day.

Although this can be a very touchy subject, please be wary of shoplifters. Yes, it's hard to believe, but there are some dishonest quilters. We have learned that there are not only retail customers who shoplift, but we received reports of vendors stealing from or doing damage to other vendor booths!

There are ways to discourage pilfering, such as putting a safety pin on some samples and threading a ribbon through the pin. Then tie the other end of the ribbon onto something stationary, such as a book rack, which will hopefully deter someone from yanking the sample off of your table and into their bag. Believe it or not, greeting and acknowledging people when they come into your booth is a good step toward discouraging shoplifters. They are counting on you being distracted and not paying attention to them.

GETTING AROUND

Depending on what and where you are vending, you will need to research and contemplate how you are going to get around. Is your everyday automobile large enough to cram everything into, or will you need something larger? If you need a larger vehicle, is it worth your while to rent a small van, or should you look into buying one? Will a trailer work for you? Can you learn how to drive with a trailer, and in particular, be able to park with a trailer?

Some people whose livelihoods are as nomadic vendors have huge recreational vehicles and a trailer for traveling from show to show.

Be sure to carefully consider the costs of any of these solutions before you make the commitment to purchase anything.

HIRING LOCAL QUILTERS TO WORK IN THE BOOTH

Sometimes local quilters can pick up a few dollars by temporarily working for some of the larger show vendors. One vendor we know of placed a small ad in a local quilt guild's newsletter, looking for help during a large local show. Of course the pay rates will vary from one vendor to another, but you could expect to earn about $10 an hour. Once the vendor establishes a working relationship with some local quilters, she can draw from these previous contacts the next time she is in town.

Chapter Fourteen
Business Issues

There are several important business issues that professional quilters should be aware of. In order to provide you with the most accurate information on each specific topic, we sought out the guidance of professionals who specialize in that particular area.

Our contributing professionals provide this information to you to use as a guide when discussing your business' needs with your own accountant, attorney, insurance agent or web designer. Every business has its own unique set of variables and must be treated as such.

<table>
<tr><td>The Importance of a Web Presence</td><td>Lyle Sandler</td></tr>
<tr><td>Establishing a Basic Web Site</td><td>Merry May</td></tr>
<tr><td>Setting up your Accounting</td><td>Kevin Meszaros, CPA</td></tr>
<tr><td>Credit Card Processing</td><td>Merry May</td></tr>
<tr><td>Insurance</td><td>Chuck Casagrande, Danskin Agency</td></tr>
<tr><td>The Business Plan/Setting Goals</td><td>Linda J. Hahn</td></tr>
<tr><td>Copyright for Quilters</td><td>Christina Manuella, Esq., Reed-Smith</td></tr>
</table>

THE IMPORTANCE OF WEB PRESENCE
by Lyle Sander

Could you imagine having access to over one billion people in the world? Well with the internet you can. This system of global interconnected computer networks provides the power to share your stories, sell your quilts and services, learn and teach. The beautiful thing is that all of the intimidating technical things are being taken care of by other people. All you have to worry about is the World Wide Web or the Web.

Just to get technical for one moment, let's understand the difference between the internet and the Web. The internet is a network of millions of interconnected computers, private and public, that are linked by wires and wireless connections as well as other more sophisticated technologies. These networks transport information such as e-mail, online chat and computer files. The World Wide Web is a system of connected documents and websites that are accessed via the internet. Web browsers, such as Internet Explorer, Apple's Safari and Firefox provide users the ability to view web pages that contain text, video, images, search fields and navigational mechanisms.

So why is it so important for quilters to use the internet? Well if you go to www.google.com and type the word "quilting" in the search field, it returns 12,700,000 results. That means that there are over 12 million pieces of information about quilting available to you.

Of course if you are planning on selling quilts or teaching people how to create quilts, the Web offers you the means to advertise your services and learn from others. All you need to do is have an internet connection, becoming another one of millions of connected people.

The best way to get connected is through your telephone company or cable television company. We highly recommend that you purchase broad-band service. This basically means you will get faster retrieval of information and the ability to use your computer as a telephone, television or radio. If cost is an issue it is better to have slower speeds than no internet connection at all.

Once you have an internet connection through your service provider, **the people who provide you with the connection to the internet – such as your telephone or cable company,** you will be able to get an e-mail address or even set up your own website. Each service provider offers a multitude of options. It is best to call their customer service number and review the options. Of course since you are now connected to the internet you could simply look up Internet Service Providers.

Let's go over some of the fundamentals. We'll start with the browser. If you are using a PC, you will have Microsoft's Internet Explorer on your computer. For those of you with Apple computers, you will have Safari. Browsers are software programs that allow you to search for and view websites. To begin, all you need to do is type an expression (group of words) in the search field and click the search button. Within seconds, you will see a plethora of information on Quilting. If you type "Quilting + New York Beauty" you will get over 2,340,000 results. Better yet, type "Quilting + New York Beauty" and select the image button above the search field on Google or Yahoo and you will get to see over 100,000 images of this veritable quilt.

We've all seen .com, .net, .biz and .org following the name of a website. These suffixes are simply parts of an internet address, not too dissimilar to your own physical address. So when you see www followed by a name and then .com or another suffix you are simply typing an address or requesting information that is sitting on a computer across town or across the globe. For general usage, .com, .net and .biz are best; .edu symbolizes an educational institution. If you go to www.register.com you will be able to check the availability of domain names. Do not be discouraged if a name you like is already taken. Be creative, but do not use a name so personal that potential customers will have to guess at what you offer.

Companies like www.coffeecup.com, www. godaddy, www.oneandone.com and www. earthlink.com have made setting up a website fairly simple. One way to judge a company's ability to serve your needs, (especially if you are a novice) is to call customer service and ask them a few questions. If they are responsive and pick up the phone quickly, you will probably be in good shape.

If you plan on engaging in e-commerce (selling your product or service on the web) you might consider hiring an experienced web designer. Type in web designer + your town name in a search box and you'll find many local people willing to help you. If you have a local design or communications school there are always students willing to make a few extra dollars to help you build a website.

As you consider designing your website, use the templates that come along with the software. They are generally easy to use and designed for maximum usability. Remember one thing; people's attention spans are very short on the web. Try to build a concise message with as few flourishes as possible.

PayPal – This is an online service that allows you to receive credit card payments over the internet without the expense major retailers incur. This has been an indispensable service for small business owners. www.paypal.com

Reciprocal Links - A Link on one website that connects to another website containing a link back to the original site. If you work with another quilter or quilt shop, they might be willing to swap links with you. This could expand your network and client base.

Website Optimization – Every word you put on your website could match a search by any person on the internet. Website optimization is the process of carefully editing and organizing your content to increase the potential for keywords to match incoming searches. Consider the language that quilters use and like – it will increase your traffic.

Blog - A blog is a contraction for web log. A blog is a website that consists of daily, relevant commentaries, musings, social interactions that often include the input of people external to your company. It's a great way to share your ideas and the ideas of your friends, co-workers and clients. Search for blogs + quilting for examples. Creating a blog is pretty simple. The company that is hosting your website will generally be able to help you set up a blog. Check out www.blogger.com.

The best thing to do is experiment. Search for things that you are passionate about. Don't be afraid. If you feel like you need a bit more, Case Western Reserve University has a good orientation to the web http://www.case.edu/help/webglossary.html. You might also want to visit http://www.2createawebsite.com .

ESTABLISHING A BASIC WEB SITE
by Merry May

There are millions of web sites in existence, and dozens more are uploaded every day. How do you set up your own web site, and what should it include?

The first step in establishing a web site is acquiring a Domain Name. This is the part of the web address that is www.YourName.com . You are not automatically committed to using the .com domain, though – there are now a number of different categories from which to choose, such as: .biz, .net, .org, and so on. Sometimes you will need to use one of these alternative categories in order to obtain the Domain Name you wish to use.

For example, if you wish to use the domain name www.YourName.com, but that domain is already registered by someone else, you may need to choose to register your Domain Name as www.YourName.net or www.YourName.biz .

The best way to find a place to register you Domain Name is through a search in your favorite search engine (such as Google) under Domain Name Registration. You will then find a whole list of places where you may register your Domain Name. Shop around and find the best deal; be sure to read the fine print, too. Also, ask questions if you don't understand the terminology or rules for that company.

All internet domains are coordinated through the Internet Corporation for Assigned Names and Numbers, or ICANN. The description on their web site states: "ICANN was formed in 1998. It is a not-for-profit public-benefit corporation with participants from all over the world dedicated to keeping the Internet secure, stable and interoperable.

It promotes competition and develops policy on the Internet's unique identifiers. ICANN doesn't control content on the Internet. It cannot stop spam and it doesn't deal with access to the Internet. But through its coordination role of the Internet's naming system, it does have an important impact on the expansion and evolution of the Internet."

Companies that offer Domain Name Registrations must be registered through ICANN and meet their standards.

As you look over the information on each of the sites that offer Domain Name Registration, you will find various offers, from a very low price per year for a certain number of years, to a "buy one get one free" offer. Again, decide what is best for you, and try to do a little research before taking the plunge. What else does that agent offer besides a low price? Do they offer free web site hosting? Do they offer an easy way for you to build your web site with templates?

Web site hosting is where a company offers to "host" or store your web site information, making it available to anyone on the internet. Hosts will often limit the amount of data they will store on your behalf, so be sure to investigate this. For example, if you have a lot of photos you wish to feature on your web site, you will want to have enough storage space for the Host to store them for you. If the Host is only offering something like 100 MB of storage space, you could quickly fill up the allotted memory with just your photos.

As far as building your actual site, the easiest way to begin is with a Host that offers Templates. A Template is a pre-programmed layout into which you simply copy and paste your information into their text or image boxes. You may use your own logo and insert it into one of the image boxes. Depending on the program being used by the Host, you may be guided step by step through the process, or you may need to be a bit more computer savvy to figure out how to upload your photos and other information. One site that we found which seems to use plain language is at :

http://www.buildwebsite4u.com/building/web-design.shtml

Another alternative is if you own a newer Macintosh computer with a program called iWeb. If you purchase a membership to their "Me.com" (formerly Mac.com), they will host your web site for you for a flat annual fee. iWeb enables you to easily build a professional looking web site using templates.

Uploading information into the Host's server simply means sending a file from your computer to the Host's computer, who then stores it and allows other people to Download the information to their own computers.

If you ultimately decide that all of this is too much work, and you have better things to do, you may also hire someone else to build your web site for you. Please see our Resources section for companies that specialize in building web sites for quilters.

At the very least, one thing you will need to do is at least organize the information you wish to present to other internet users. One helpful way of doing this is by using an outline format. This will help you to categorize your information so it is accessible and not too confusing for visitors to your site to navigate. You might also wish to visit the web sites of other quilt professionals to see how their information is organized. You may not copy another web site's images without permission, though, because this is a violation of copyright law. We are including a sample outline for a web

site below, beginning with the all-important Home Page.

DOMAIN NAME: www.YourName.com

A. Home Page: This is the central point where people will be directed when they are looking for information about you. It is similar to the Table of Contents in a book. It should include links to all of the other major categories on your web site. A "page" is each individual portion of a web site. There can be only one page, or hundreds of them, depending on the amount of information you wish to provide. Keep in mind, however, that the more pages you have on your web site, the more your hosting fees will be, because your host is storing more information for you.

B. About: You may wish to have a photo of yourself on this page; it is mainly a page summarizing your career, and giving a brief synopsis of how you arrived at your current point in your career. This is similar to the "About the Author" page in a book. It may also contain information about how to contact you. We strongly suggest not including your home address or telephone number on this page, because it can lead to some unwanted attention from time to time. You could include the state you live in and your e-mail; perhaps even a special e-mail address such as: info@YourName.com. Check with your Host to see if e-mail addresses are included in their hosting. If you have a Resumé, you may wish to include a link to it here as an optional download.

C. Your Specialty: This can be anything from a list of your workshops and lectures, to photos of your award winning quilts, to samples of commission work you have completed in the past. This page should be all about the kind of work you do, and what you specialize in. It is somewhat like a visual resumé. From the individual parts of this page, you may add Links to other pages with more details about your work. For example, you may have a list of your workshops here, with links to individual pages with more detailed information and photos. A "link" is a shortcut which allows you to quickly travel from one page to another.

D. Photo Gallery: You may include photos of things such as your work, your work space, and brief descriptions of each photo. Many programs will allow your visitors to click on an image to enlarge it for easier viewing of the details. This is similar to an online Portfolio of your work.

E. Favorite Links: At some point you will begin to gather requests from other people with web sites to "trade links." This simply means adding a link on your page to allow your viewers to explore another web site. In exchange, the other web site owner includes a link back to your own web site. It is good "netiquette" to request permission from other web site owners before you add a link on your site to their site.

F. Contact Us: Although this may seem a bit redundant if you have an "About" page, many people will look for an easy way to contact you. Again, we recommend using an e-mail address, or better yet, the words "Contact Us" which have a link to your e-mail address. This helps to cut down on the amount of "spam" or junk e-mails which are gathered by search engines, causing you to receive numerous e-mails about how to increase the size of your _____ (fill in the blank!), or how to lose weight. With a link to your e-mail through "Contact Us", the visitor to your site will be required to actually click on the link to your e-mail, therefore eliminating much of the unwanted spam.

You should be consistent about including links to all of your other pages within your web site at the top of each page, the bottom of each page, or along the left side of each page. This allows visitors to quickly navigate from one page to another, or to return to the previous page they were viewing on your site.

Another thing you might consider is establishing your own Blog, or weB Log. These are sites which allow you to share stories about your work, details about what you are currently working on, and photos. Other viewers may be able to post comments about your site or upload their own photos. Please see our Resources section for some links to established Blog sites.

SETTING UP YOUR ACCOUNTING
by Kevin Meszaros, CPA

As a CPA in the state of New Jersey for nearly 35 years I have built a practice that consists primarily of small businesses and individual tax returns. Throughout the years the questions from small business owners have remained the same. Here are some of the most frequently asked questions when starting up a business:

Q. What are my choices of business structure when starting my small business?

A. The following are the various forms of business structures:

1. Sole Proprietor
2. Partnership
3. Corporation
4. Limited Liability Company

The differences between these entities mainly deal with liability exposure and reporting requirements. You should consult with your personal tax advisor for help with choosing the type that is best for you since he or she will be most familiar with your individual situation.

Q. How do I set up a method of tracking the income and expenses of my small business?

A. There are various methods of bookkeeping for business income and expenses including:

1. A pre-printed bookkeeping journal, which can be purchased at most business supply stores.
2. Column and lined accounting paper, using separate sheets for income and expenses.
3. One-write checkbook, a checkbook that records the expenditure on a journal sheet when it is written by way of a carbon strip on the back of the check. It is also attached to a columned spreadsheet that allows you to categorize the expenses.
4. Computer based accounting programs can be used. There are several low cost options for small businesses such as Quicken for Business, QuickBooks and Peachtree. All of these programs are user-friendly and provide tutorial help for set up.

Q. What kind of expenses am I allowed to deduct?

A. This is the most common question that is asked by someone starting up or operating a business. Business expenses fall into certain categories.

1. Cost of Goods Sold – If your business manufactures products such as quilts or purchases them from others to be resold to the general public you generally must value your inventory on hand at the beginning and the end of each tax year to determine your cost of goods sold. The value of the Cost of Goods Sold is deducted from your gross receipts to determine your gross profit for the year. This includes all of the items that are directly involved in producing quilts such as fabric, thread and other supplies. If your business is service related, such as quilting instruction, and there is no product involved, then you do not need to be concerned with Cost of Goods Sold.

2. Capital Expenses – these costs must be capitalized and cannot be fully deducted in the year in which they were incurred. They must be amortized or depreciated over multiple tax periods. In general there are three types of costs you capitalize.

i. Business start up costs: the cost incurred in forming and starting your business. I.E: registration or incorporation fees, legal fees, etc.

ii. Business assets: the cost of equipment. I.E.: sewing machines, display cases, office furniture, etc.

iii. Improvements: these are the costs of changes to your business location whether you operate from your home or you rent an outside space. This includes items such as putting up walls and ceilings, making changes to your electrical service, etc.

3. Operating Expenses – the following is a list of some of the most common expenses you can deduct:

- Advertising Costs
- Association dues and membership fees
- Insurance
- Business interest expense
- Legal and accounting fees
- Office supplies and expenses
- Rent
- Repairs and maintenance
- Supplies
- Licenses
- Taxes
- Travel expenses
- Meals and entertainment
- Utilities
- Business telephone usage
- Tradeshow expenses
- Free samples
- Business literature
- Sponsorship fees
- Trade publications and magazines
- Continuing education courses
- Travel expenses
- Website expenses
- Business computer expenses

This is just a partial list of the more common business expenses you can deduct. For a more complete list and for guidance on all the types of deductible expenses please refer to Publication 535 – Business Expenses. This Publication can be downloaded for free at the IRS website IRS.gov. You can also obtain a copy from your local IRS Service Center.

Q. If I operate my business out of my home can I deduct any expenses?

A. If you use part of your home for business, you may be able to deduct expenses for the business use of your home. These expenses may include mortgage interest, insurance, utilities, repairs and depreciation.

For further information on how to deduct these expenses please refer to IRS Publication 587 – Business Use of Your Home.

Q. If I use my car for business can I deduct the expenses of operating it?

A. If you use your car for your business you can deduct your expenses. If you use your car for both business and personal purposes, you must choose between two methods to deduct expenses. Under the first method you must divide your expenses based on the actual business miles driven for the year divided by the total mileage driven for the year.

Under the second method the government allows a standard mileage rate, which is multiplied by the business miles driven for the year. The mileage rate takes into account fuel, insurance, repairs, registration and depreciation. As of the date of this publication the standard mileage rate for business is 58.5 cents per mile. This rate is adjusted periodically to reflect the change in fuel costs and other operating expenses.

For further information please refer to IRS Publication 463 – Travel, Entertainment, Gift and Car Expenses.

The preceding questions should get you started setting up your business from a financial and tax perspective. If you feel confident that you understand how these items relate to your business, then you should have no problem. However, if you have any doubt I suggest that you consult a tax professional for help in preparing your business taxes since he or she is trained to deal with a variety of businesses.

CREDIT CARD PROCESSING
By Merry May

When you are ready to take the plunge into credit card processing, you need to know some of the ins and outs, as well as some of the potential pitfalls.

When I first decided I needed to accept credit cards, it was when I was a vendor at quilt shows.

I had no one I could ask for advice on establishing a merchant's account, what the fees were, and how much the processing equipment would cost. At first, I approached my local bank, but decided the minimum sales requirements were too high. So I called the toll-free number on my own credit card, and made an inquiry.

The company sent me an application, which I completed and mailed to them along with the required documentation. After a few weeks, I was accepted as a merchant, and was sent information about my monthly minimum sales requirement, percentages per sale, transaction fees (including monthly statement fees), and the option to either lease or purchase my processing equipment.

I decided it would be less expensive in the long run to purchase my equipment, which cost about $1,000 (processor and printer).

Because I knew my sales volume would be somewhat low at the beginning, I was willing to pay a higher percentage for each sale than most businesses pay. I was happy just to be able to accept credit card sales!

Little did I know that these percentages and many of the fees are very negotiable! It wasn't until I decided that the monthly fees were too much that the company offered to lower my percentages. I was not a happy camper, after paying too much for all that time!

Through a fellow merchant I eventually discovered that I could pay a small annual fee, plus a small percentage and a relatively small transaction fee, and be able to process credit cards online. No more statement fees, no hassles, life is good.

I now use this service for all of my processing needs, including commission work sales. It is easy to use, the funds clear within about two days, and there are no hidden fees to worry about. Once the funds have cleared through the processor, I transfer them directly into my business checking account. This way I know exactly how much money is in my account, because I put it there myself. With my former processors, they were constantly moving money in and out of my account: sales going in, percentages and fees going out. I had no idea how much money I really had, and settling my checkbook each month was a nightmare.

One of the major concerns with processing credit cards, especially for online sales, is the presence of fraud, mostly through stolen credit cards or identity theft. You need to be aware that fraudulent sales can happen to anyone who processes credit cards. However, with some due diligence you can certainly reduce the likelihood of a "chargeback."

A chargeback happens when a person sees an unfamiliar charge on their credit card statement. They call their credit card company and dispute the charge. The credit card company then contacts the merchant, who must prove that the charge was legitimate. There is paperwork to complete within a short period of time. If the credit card company is satisfied with your response, the charge will stay as it is. If they are not satisfied, then there will be a chargeback on your account. This means they will immediately deduct the charge (plus a transaction fee, and perhaps a penalty as well) from your checking account, and credit the original amount back to the card holder.

As you can see, you want to avoid going through a chargeback. It costs you valuable time researching the original sale, recalling who placed the order, and lots of other headaches. In addition, it leaves a bad mark on your merchant account.

If you receive a sale online from an overseas address, especially if it is for a large amount, and the billing address is far different from the shipping address, approach it with caution! If you are uncertain about the legitimacy of a sale, contact your credit card processing company and ask them to make an inquiry about the owner of the card. Is the person traveling in a foreign country, or is it just their credit card information that decided to go on a spending spree?

Although credit card sales can greatly increase your bottom line, you are ultimately responsible for verifying the customer's identity before you process a credit card.

INSURANCE
by Chuck Casagranda, Danskin Agency

A TRAVELING QUILT TEACHER

Travel entails different exposures to an object that has notable value. If a quilt is normally located in a museum for example, on display day after day in the same building and the same room, the risks of damage, destruction, conversion, etc. are quantifiable. An insurance underwriter

evaluates the exposure to loss based on the following: construction of the building (frame, joisted masonry, non combustible, etc.), the occupancy of the premises (museum, commercial operation, other public building such as a school, etc.), the protection at that premises (sprinklered or not, fire/smoke/or burglary alarm, and is that alarm local, alerts the police or is monitored by a central station 24 hours a day?) Finally, what are the adjacent exposures to this location? Is there a restaurant in the same building without firewall separation? Is there a hazardous manufacturing occupancy next door that may have a far greater likelihood of sustaining a property loss thereby affecting the risk of loss to a quilt?

These conditions apply to a quilt that usually is located in one place. Travel entails changing risk as it is difficult to evaluate the exposure to loss as these exposures can frequently change or may simply be unknown. A quilt traveling in a vehicle is exposed to the transportation risks associated with driving. A car may be involved in a collision with another vehicle or a collision with a large animal such as a deer. Vehicles sometimes are stolen (thus losing the contents of that vehicle) and have been known to catch fire and be incinerated. If traveling by common carrier such as a train or plane, in addition to the transportation risks enumerated above, there are the additional risks of theft by a member of the public or the mishandling or loss of a quilt that is handled as baggage.

When the destination is reached, there are new exposures to deal with as the quilt has arrived at a new location that has its own set of hazards. There may not even be a building to evaluate as was done above but rather simply a "location" where the quilt will temporarily be situated.

The insurance industry solution to this transient exposure is a type of policy called a "fine arts floater." The floater policy is a type of inland marine contract that insures against most types of loss and is typically written on a "valued basis." Valued policies are not that common in the insurance industry as most property type policies are written on a replacement cost or actual cash value (this assumes depreciation or sometimes obsolescence). In a valued policy, the owner of the object being insured (the quilt or quilts) and the insurance carrier agree BEFORE ANY LOSS OCCURS the value of the object. Thus, if and when a covered loss happens, the valuation of the quilt is already established and the insuror pays the value that the quilt was insured for. This is not true of most other insurance contracts as the replacement value or the actual cash value of an insured property is DETERMINED AT THE TIME OF THE LOSS.

The distinction is important as one of the difficulties in insuring a quilt is establishing a value that the owner and the insurance underwriter agree on at the initial writing of the floater policy. One method is to obtain a qualified appraisal to determine the value of the quilt. The appraiser must be acceptable to the insurance underwriter and this may be another obstacle to overcome in obtaining the proper insurance. The underwriter must be convinced that the selected appraiser has the experience and background to knowledgeably determine the proper value of a quilt.

TEACHERS IN GENERAL

Aside from the risk of damage to one's own property, there is always the potential to cause damage to another person or their property. Insurance carriers offer commercial liability coverage to protect against these types of exposures. Specifically, the insurance provides protection for the insured against personal and advertising injury, bodily injury and property damage. Personal and advertising injury in insurance parlance, encompasses the "intentional torts" of false arrest, detention or imprisonment; malicious prosecution; wrongful eviction; wrongful entry or invasion of right of private occupancy; libel, slander, defamation of character; violation of a person's privacy; use of another's idea in your advertisement; copyright, trade dress or slogan infringement.

More common are the bodily injury and property damage claims that arise from everyday activities or conditions. A slip and fall can be caused by a condition (spilled coffee that was not cleaned up in a timely manner) within the control of a teacher. In addition, an activity by the teacher (bumping into someone) can also cause bodily injury to a person.

Property damage to property of others is subject to similar exposures as described under bodily injury claims. There is one further caution with respect to property damage claims, namely, the "care, custody and control" exclusion in commercial liability policies. This exclusion eliminates liability coverage for property the insured has in their care, custody or control. Further discussion of how to deal with this exclusion will be included in the Long Arm Quilter Discussion.

LONG ARM QUILTERS

A person or business that takes in property of others to modify, clean or store is referred to as a "bailee" of that property. The most common example is that of a dry cleaner that accepts articles of clothing from the public to clean, repair, etc. The dry cleaner has a legal obligation to use due care while possessing property of others. The degree of care is commensurate with the type of bailee and in the dry cleaner example we are dealing with a commercial bailment. This type of bailee owes a much higher degree of care than a gratuitous bailment such as one's neighbor requesting them to watch their dog for free while that neighbor takes a vacation for a week. The commercial kennel that charges for boarding services would owe the highest degree of care for property of others in their control.

A long arm quilter takes in quilts from others in various stages of completion and adds value to that quilt by finishing the quilting stitches. In this situation, a commercial bailment is created and a high degree of care is owed to the owner of the quilt submitted for finishing. To protect against this exposure, the insurance industry over time has developed bailee's coverage for the property in one's care. However, this doesn't necessarily require that two policies be carried by long arm quilters, one for owned quilts and a separate bailee's policy for the quilts taken in. Property of others can typically be written on fine arts floaters in addition to owned property. Care should be exercised in the purchase of floater coverage as some insurance carriers exclude repair, restoration or retouching. Floater policies are not standardized forms and may vary from company to company. It is advisable to find a knowledgeable insurance agent and work with that individual to tailor coverage for each situation.

VENDING

Individuals who travel from show to show to market their goods should consider a floater policy for their inventory. Also, commercial liability is available to protect against operational and premises hazards such as trips and falls. In addition, products liability is usually included in commercial liability and protects against bodily injury or property damage caused by a product sold by a business. The products exposure for quilters may appear to be modest, but there is always the possibility of bodily injury or damage to other's property. An example could be a purchaser of a quilt that sustains an allergic reaction to the materials used in a quilt.

The aforementioned property and liability coverage can usually be combined into a "package policy" that has great flexibility in adding different coverage elements. Coverage such as business interruption, that will be discussed later, can be added to the package policy along with a number of other business coverage.

DISABILITY INSURANCE

Disability income protection is sold on both a group and individual basis to those applicants whose income is verifiable and sustainable. This coverage is purchased to replace a portion of an individual's income that is either curtailed or stopped due to the inability to work and earn income. The definition of disability in an insurance contract is very important and will determine just when the policyholder is considered disabled and thereby eligible for benefits under the policy. Other important elements of a disability contract are the terms "non cancellable and guaranteed renewable." These terms provide that the disability policy can only be cancelled by the insured as long as the premium is paid and the premium cannot be raised by the insurance company during the lifetime of the policy (e.g.

disability policies that run to age 65).

Disability Income policies are rated on the applicant's age, occupation (a miner would expect to pay more than a quilter) and general health. The amount of monthly income an applicant qualifies for is typically not more than 50% of that applicant's gross monthly income. Policies are sometime sold for a two or five year term or to age sixty five. There is almost always a waiting period in the policy before a coverage disability commences paying the purchased monthly income amount, ranging from thirty days to six months. All these factors are considered when qualifying for disability income insurance.

BUSINESS INTERRUPTION INSURANCE

Property losses sustained by a business are oftentimes categorized as direct or indirect. Direct losses are damage to tangible property such as a building, contents of a building, etc. Indirect losses are events such as loss of income that is a result of direct loss to a building or other tangible property. There are a considerable number of businesses that fail to reopen their doors after a direct loss because they did not have protection against indirect losses. That protection is referred to as business income coverage.

Business income coverage is designed to replace the income that would have been earned by a business during the time repairs are being made (or a total rebuild is being done). After a covered property loss, two important questions should be answered to determine what is the projected loss of income. The first is to establish how long it will take to repair or rebuild the property to the pre loss condition. The second is what is the actual

loss of earnings that would have been earned in that time period.

These questions also illustrate the difficulty in establishing the proper amount of business income insurance to purchase before a loss occurs. Is the business seasonal? If so, the timing of a property loss will greatly affect the projected loss sustained. What expenses do not continue after the occurrence of a property loss? Many leases for real property excuse the payment of rent if the premises occupied becomes untenable because of a physical loss. What about notes on equipment or real property (mortgage)? These debt obligations typically continue, or worse, most mortgages become due & payable upon the destruction on the liened property. One must also consider the "time element" of how long will it take to repair or replace the property?

There are somewhat complicated business income worksheets that some insurance underwriters require of applicants in order to justify and establish the proper amount of insurance to carry. The help of an accountant that understands one's business is a considerable help in securing the proper insurance to value.

CONCLUSION

Insurance contracts are regulated state by state and are not necessarily the same in every jurisdiction. There is some uniformity in the use of "standard industry forms" such as those promulgated by organizations like The Insurance Service Offices (ISO). ISO forms are in common use around the country for commercial liability. This makes a comparison among insurance carriers easier if they are utilizing the same coverage form. The comparison becomes more difficult when non standardized forms are used such as is usual for fine arts floaters. An astute business person will seek the assistance of a seasoned insurance agent that will work with the client in understanding the business exposures and tailoring the appropriate protection program. It may be boring, but try to read the policy form to understand just what protection is provided.

YOUR BUSINESS PLAN/SETTING GOALS
by Linda J. Hahn

As you begin planning your new business, we would highly suggest that you write out a Business Plan or at the very least, maintain a notebook which contains the goals you wish to accomplish and how you plan to get there.

A Google search for "Business Plan Template" will yield many sites which offer free templates for you to adapt to your individual business. There are also some software programs which will assist you in writing your plan.

Presenting a business plan when attempting to secure a small business loan will demonstrate to your loan officer that you are serious and have thought your ideas through.

A few of the websites we have found include:

> www.score.org
> www.microsoft.com
> www.bplans.com
> www.myownbusiness.com

Your business plan should include:

- A cover page with your company name and logo (if you have one).
- A table of contents
- Overview (summary of what you plan to do)

- Business Background (skills and experience)
- Marketing Plan (how and where you will advertise and the cost involved)
- Action Plan (details on what you plan do to and how you will accomplish same)
- Financial Management Statement (current status, projections, costs)
- Closing

If you do not wish to write out a Business Plan, a toned down version could be in the way of a Goal Statement. A goal statement is simply that - what you want to accomplish and the time frame in which you wish to accomplish the goal. You can write down your projections for one year, three years and five years from now.

You may wish to start a small group with some quilt professional colleagues. You can decide how often to meet to discuss your individual goals and collectively brainstorm how you can achieve them.

Michele Scott recently told us that she just found (and reviewed) her goal statement that she made in 1999, at the first Quilt Professionals' Network Retreat she attended. She relayed (quite proudly) that she had accomplished all the goals she had set for herself several years ago.

THE LEGAL PROTECTIONS AVAILABLE TO QUILT DESIGNERS AND INSTRUCTORS UNDER THE COPYRIGHT ACT
By Christina Manuelli, Esq.

The Copyright Act of 1976, as amended to date (U.S.C. 17 §101 et seq.) (to be referred to in this chapter as the "Copyright Act"), is a federal law which grants certain exclusive rights to the copyright owners that create copyrightable works. Quilters who create original quilt designs and who fix those designs into a tangible form are entitled to the protections afforded to their works of original authorship by the Copyright Act. Among other protections, the Copyright Act protects quilters against the unauthorized copying of their copyrighted original designs as well as the unauthorized creation of similar, infringing designs.

Basic Concepts of Copyright Law

The Copyright Act extends its protections to eight categories of "works of authorship" (U.S.C. 17 §102), including literary works; musical works; dramatic works; pantomimes and choreographic works; pictorial, graphic and sculptural works; motion pictures and other audiovisual works; sound recordings; and architectural works. A quilt design is copyrightable because it is a pictorial work, provided that such quilt design also meets the Copyright Act's requirements that such work be (i) original and (ii) fixed in a tangible medium from which it can be perceived, reproduced or otherwise communicated. In the case of a quilt which can also serve a utilitarian purpose as a blanket, copyright protection only extends to the artistic elements and not to its utilitarian aspects.

In order for the work to be original, a quilt design must not be a copy of another work.

In order for a quilt design to meet the requirement of having been "fixed into a tangible medium", such design must be placed into a form that can be seen or reproduced. In other words, the design could be sketched onto paper or stitched together with pieces of fabric. Similarly, original instructional materials authored by a quilter must be put into writing before

those materials are protected by copyright. The mere idea or concept of a design that a quilter may have in his or her head is not copyrightable until that quilter places that idea or concept into a form that can be seen or otherwise perceived.

The Exclusive Rights of the Copyright Owner

Subject to certain limitation stated in the Copyright Act, including, but not limited to the right of "fair use" (discussed below), the owner of copyright in a pictorial work, such as a quilt design, has the exclusive rights to do and to authorize any of the following:

(1) to reproduce the copyrighted work in copies;

(2) to prepare derivative works based upon the copyrighted work;

(3) to distribute copies of the copyrighted work to the public by sale or other transfer of ownership, or by rental, lease or lending; and

(4) to display the copyrighted work publicly.

See U.S.C. 17 §106. The Copyright Act also vests the exclusive right to perform certain works in the copyright owner, but those rights do not arise with respect to quilt designs or instructional materials.

The term "*exclusive*" in this context means that only the copyright owner may exercise those rights, and therein lies the essential value of copyright. Subject to a few exceptions under the law, such as "fair use", the copyright owner can control who has the right to reproduce, distribute, display or create derivative works based upon his or her work. If a third party wrongfully exercises the rights of the copyright owner without permission or without a license, an "*infringement*" of copyright has occurred and the copyright owner will have certain remedies available to him or her under the law to enforce and seek redress for those rights.

Who holds the Copyright in a Work?

As a general rule, copyright in a work protected by the Copyright Act vests initially in the author or joint authors of the work. Therefore, the quilter who creates an original quilt design is automatically vested with the exclusive rights described above from the time of the design's creation.

An exception to the general rule stated above arises with respect to "*works made for hire*", which category of works includes, but is not limited to, works prepared by an employee within the scope of his or her employment.[1] In that case, the employer for whom the work was prepared will be the copyright owner. For example, if Susan Smith is an employee of Quilting Designs, Inc. and she creates a quilt design within the scope of her employment, her employer, Quilting Designs, Inc., will own the copyright in that design.

What is the term of copyright?

The term of copyright is the period during which the copyright owner holds and can exercise his or her exclusive rights in that work. It is also the period during which third parties cannot rightfully exercise those exclusive rights in that work unless the copyright owner has given permission for such use, the copyright owner has assigned some or all of his exclusive rights to that third party or such use is permitted without the copyright owner's permission under the principles of "*fair use*" (see discussion below).

Copyright in a work created on or after January 1, 1978, subsists from the time of its creation, regardless of whether that work

is published or not. Generally, in the case of a work that is created by a single person after January 1, 1978, copyright in that work will continue for the life of the author plus seventy (70) years after the author's death. In the case of a joint work created by one or more authors, copyright in that joint work will continue for a term of the life of the last surviving author plus seventy (70) years after such last surviving author's death.

The law also provides that the term of copyright will run through December 31st of the calendar year in which the term of copyright is due to expire.

For example, if Mary Doe completes the creation of an original quilt design on January 1, 2009, and if she dies on May 1, 2029, the term of copyright in Mary's quilt design will continue for 70 years after her death through December 31, 2099. The copyright owner will become the Estate of Mary Doe and then copyright will vest under the terms of her will in another person or entity, but the new copyright owner will not be able to extend the term of copyright in Mary's quilt design beyond December 31, 2099. On January 1, 2100, Mary's quilt design will be in the public domain.

For works that were created prior to January 1, 1978, and other specific types of works, the duration of copyright is computed differently. For "works made for hire" (including works made by an employee within the scope of his or her employment), the copyright endures for a term of 95 years from the date of the work's first publication or for a term of 120 years, whichever term expires first.

Once the term of copyright expires, the work falls into the "*public domain*," which means that anyone may rightfully make and distribute copies of that work or create derivative works based upon that work without violating the copyright of the copyright owner. Certain traditional block patterns commonly used in quilt designs that were developed many years ago are within the public domain, which means that those patterns can be copied or modified without infringing any person's copyright.

Who has the right to copy or modify a copyrighted quilt design?

The copyright owner has the exclusive right to reproduce his or her copyrighted quilt design. With the exception of "fair use" (explained below), no one else has the authority or the right to copy that quilt design without the copyright owner's permission.

The same is true with respect to the right to modify a copyrighted quilt design. The copyright owner has the exclusive right to create derivative works based upon her original design. A modified version of an original quilt design is a "*derivative work*" because it has been taken from or "derived" from the original version. An original quilt design is composed of many elements—the shapes of the pieces, how the pieces fit together, the stitching patterns or techniques, the dimensions, the colors, patterns. The way that all of those elements are combined into a single design is what makes it original. A third party cannot simply change one or two of those elements and claim copyright in that modified version without infringing the copyright owner's rights.

The express grant of the authority

to exercise any of the exclusive rights of copyright is called a "*license.*" A third party who wants to reproduce a copyrighted quilt design or create a modified version of that original design must obtain a license to do so from the copyright owner. If that third party fails to obtain the copyright owner's permission, the unauthorized copy or the unauthorized derivative work constitutes an infringement of the copyright owner's rights.

Fair Use

Section 107 of the Copyright Act states that the "*fair use*" of a copyrighted work, including reproduction, for the limited purposes of criticism, comment, news reporting, teaching (including multiple copies for classroom use), scholarship, or research does not constitute an infringement of copyright. Section 107 also lists four factors that should be considered in determining whether a particular use of a copyright work constitutes a fair use:

(1) the purpose and character of the use, including whether such use is of a commercial nature or is for nonprofit educational purposes;

(2) the nature of the copyrighted work;

(3) the amount and substantiality of the portion used in relation to the copyrighted work as a whole; and

(4) the effect of the use upon the potential market for or value of the copyrighted work.

The issue of fair use usually arises in the context of an alleged copyright

---

[1]The definition of the term "works made for hire" found in the Copyright Act also includes works created by an independent contractor, provided that the work falls within one of the nine categories listed in such definition and there is a written agreement between the independent contractor and the party who commissioned the work that specifies that the work is to be considered a "work made for hire." Quilt designs do not generally fall into any of those nine categories. For more information, see Circular 9 of the U.S. Copyright Office, "Works Made for Hire Under the 1976 Copyright Act."

infringement. For example, instead of denying the alleged unauthorized reproduction of a copyright work, the person who is accused of copyright infringement raises fair use as a defense against the claims of the copyright owner. The determination of whether such use constituted a fair use or a copyright infringement is made by a trial judge who will apply the factors listed above to the particular facts of the case.

Fair use is a heavily litigated area of copyright law. Because it is a fact-sensitive issue, there are no hard and fast rules for what constitutes fair use. Within the quilter's world, this issue may arise in the following contexts:

• First example: A copy of a quilt design may be displayed or distributed by the instructor to students for instructional purposes.

• Second example: Written instructional materials may be distributed by the author to students in a quilting class, and those students later make additional copies and re-distribute them to other quilters.

• Third example: A photographer takes a photo of a copyrighted quilt design at a trade show without the copyright owner's permission and then includes the photograph in a commercially published book of quilt designs.

• Fourth example: A retailer copies and sells copyrighted quilt design patterns without the quilt designer's permission.

In the first example, a key factor for consideration would be whether the class was offered in a nonprofit setting, such as a class given to senior citizens as part of a community support program. In the second example, a key factor might be whether the students charged others for the materials and whether they used the copied materials to compete with the instructor. In the third and fourth examples, the commercial nature of the use by the photographer or the retailer and the detrimental effect upon the quilt designer—denying her royalties from the reproductions of her copyrighted designs-- would likely weigh heavily against a finding of fair use and in favor of a finding of infringement.

The best way to avoid a claim of infringement is to obtain the permission of the copyright owner in advance of using the copyrighted material. If permission is granted, get it in writing!

The Concept of Divisible Rights

A very important concept to understand about copyright is that each of the exclusive rights of the copyright owner can be divided and subdivided. Copyright is often compared to a bundle of sticks, with each stick representing one of the exclusive rights listed above. The copyright owner can hold onto the entire bundle of sticks and never allow any other person to exercise any of those exclusive rights. On the other hand, the copyright owner could also sell or transfer the entire bundle of sticks to a third party who would then become the copyright owner, and the original creator of the work would no longer be entitled to exercise any of those exclusive rights. The more usual case is that the copyright owner will give away only one or a few of those sticks on a limited, "*nonexclusive*" basis. "*Nonexclusive*" means that the same rights can be granted by the copyright owner to another party, as well as exercised by the copyright owner.

For example, the copyright owner of a quilt design could choose never to permit any person to copy that quilt design, but that would limit his income to the sale of finished quilts made by him. Also, by refusing to allow a third party to copy that design, the copyright owner could be increasing the risk of an infringement. Instead, that same copyright owner could grant a limited, nonexclusive license to a third party to make five copies of that quilt design in exchange for a fee. As a result, the copyright owner has generated income, he has retained the full right to reproduce the copyrighted design, and he also has the right to sell other nonexclusive licenses to other parties.

It is also important to understand that each exclusive right can be broken down and divided among multiple persons. In other words, it is not necessary to give the entire stick to a single third party. For example, a copyright owner of a quilt design could grant the owner of a retail craft supply store the nonexclusive right to display the design in her privately-owned store; at the same time, the copyright owner could also grant the owner of a gift store the nonexclusive right to display the same quilt design in her window. Because those rights are nonexclusive, the copyright owner still holds the right to publicly display her quilt design. Think of it as the copyright owner dividing the stick representing the exclusive right to publicly display her work into smaller sticks, while still holding onto a large piece of the original stick.

See the discussion below entitled **"Practical Licensing Tips"** for suggestions on how a copyright owner can protect his or her rights in an original quilt design or instructional materials while reaping future economic or artistic benefits.

Protecting Your Copyright

There are several simple, inexpensive ways for a copyright owner to protect his or her copyrights. These steps are particularly important once a work is published. A quilt design is first published when copies of it are distributed to the public by sale, lease or lending. Simply displaying a quilt design in a public place does not constitute publication.

In short, to protect your original quilt design or training materials, the following steps are recommended:

- Put a copyright notice on all copies of your original work, whether it is published or unpublished.

- Register your original work with the U.S. Copyright Office.

- Put any permissions or licenses to use your work in writing.

- Before you grant permission or a license assigning broad or exclusive rights in your original work, seek legal advice! If you don't understand the rights that are being granted, do not sign it. Legal advice may be available to you from a local chapter of lawyers that provide services on a pro bono basis to artists or artisans in your community.

Copyright Notices

United States copyright laws used to require that, as a pre-condition to enjoying the benefits of copyright protection, the published copies of a work bear a copyright notice. The law changed in 1989 when the Copyright Act was revised. The current law does not require that all published copies bear a copyright notice in order for a copyright owner to enjoy the protections afforded by copyright. Nevertheless, placing a copyright notice on a published work has definite benefits: A copyright notice puts the world on notice that a particular work is protected by the Copyright Act and it identifies the copyright owner. Furthermore, if a work bearing a copyright notice is infringed, the infringer cannot raise a defense of innocent infringement, claiming that he or she did not know that the work was protected. For those reasons, a copyright notice should be placed on all copies of original quilt designs (including on the quilt itself), as well as on original training materials.

Forms of Copyright Notice for a Published Work: The notice should contain the following three elements: (i) the word Copyright or the symbol ©, followed by (ii) the year of first publication of the work, followed by the name of the copyright owner or an abbreviation of the name by which the name can be recognized.

For example, if Linda Hahn created a quilt design, any copies of that design (in fabric or paper form) that she distributes to the public in 2009 should bear the following copyright notice:

Copyright 2009 Linda Hahn

Another acceptable form of copyright notice for a published work would be:

© 2009 Linda Hahn

Form of Notice for an Unpublished Work: It is not necessary to place a copyright notice on an unpublished work, but it would be wise to do so if copies of the copyrighted work leave the control of the copyright owner. For example, if a quilt is to be displayed in an area where photographs could be taken of the copyrighted design, placing a notice on the quilt would leave no doubt that copyright in that work is claimed. The form of notice for an unpublished work would be:

Unpublished Work © Merry May

If in doubt, put your copyright notice on your original work. It tells the world who holds the copyright and to use caution before reproducing the work without permission.

Copyright Registration

The Copyright Act provides for registration of copyrightable works with the U. S. Copyright Office in Washington, D.C. Registration is not a condition of copyright protection. However, if a copyright owner wants to bring a suit for copyright infringement, the work that is the subject of that claim must be registered before a lawsuit may be commenced. If registration is made within three months after the first publication of the work, the copyright owner, if he or she prevails in an infringement action, may be entitled to receive statutory damages (an amount of damages set by the statute with no need for the copyright owner to prove actual damages) and/or attorney's fees.

Procedures for Copyright Registration: A quilt design should be registered as a work of visual art. Instructional materials should be registered as a literary work. In order to register a work, an application for registration, a filing fee and a "deposit" must be submitted to the U.S. Copyright Office.

The application form can be downloaded from the U.S. Copyright Office website or submitted online. The filing fee as of July 1, 2008 is $35 for an online registration and $45 for submission of a paper form. In view of the benefits that the registration can bring, it is a relatively inexpensive investment to protect your rights in an original work that could bring significant commercial benefits to the copyright owner.

The deposit is a *complete copy* of the work to be registered. If an author were applying for registration of a book, she would submit a complete copy of the text of the book. For a visual work, such as a quilt design, "identifying material" showing the visual work must be submitted. A photograph, a photocopy or a drawing of the complete copyrightable content of the quilt design should be submitted. If color or a particular fabric pattern is an important original element of the design, be sure to submit a deposit copy that is in color. It should also be kept in mind that the deposit copy is retained by the Copyright Office. For more information on how to submit a proper deposit, see the U.S. Copyright Circular 40A, available on the website listed below as a helpful resource.

For Assistance with Copyright Registration Questions. The U.S. Copyright Office has a very-user friendly website which includes all the needed forms, filing fee schedules and instructions for filing a copyright registration. See http://www.copyright.gov. This website also contains helpful publications on numerous general and specific topics. Under the "Contact Us" link, there is an email address as well as a telephone number that allows copyright questions to be directed to a member of the Copyright Office staff. Under the "Registration" link, there is also an online tutoring on how to file an online copyright registration.

The "Poor Man's Copyright": There is a myth about copyright protection known as the "poor man's copyright". Instead of obtaining a copyright registration from the U.S. Copyright Office by following the procedures described above and paying the appropriate filing fees, the myth suggests that the author should place his work in a sealed envelope and then mail the envelope to himself through the postal service. When the package arrives, the author should then keep the unopened envelope as evidence of his authorship and as evidence of the date of creation. The U.S. Copyright Office website states specifically that this practice is

not recognized by the Copyright Act and is no substitute for registration. As mentioned above, in the event of an infringement claim, the value of a valid copyright registration could far exceed the cost of a registration. With so many resources available through the U.S. Copyright website, including the ability to communicate with staff members, at no additional cost, copyright registration is a relatively inexpensive way to maximize the legal protections available to the owner of an original work.

Licenses or Permissions to Reproduce

As mentioned above in the section captioned "**Who has the right to copy or modify a copyrighted quilt design?**", unless the right of fair use applies, any third party that desires to exercise any of the exclusive rights of the copyright owner must obtain permission to do so. The grant of such rights by the copyright owner is also called a "*license*".

Practical Licensing Tips

As mentioned above, there are many different ways to divide, and subdivide, the bundle of exclusive rights held by a copyright owner. All of the possibilities are too numerous to discuss in this summary. With the bundle of sticks analogy in mind, the following simple rules of thumb should help guide the copyright owner when making decisions that would affect his or her exclusive rights in the copyrighted work:

- Be careful as the copyright owner to retain the greatest amount of rights for future use as desired. In other words, do not give away exclusive rights that you, as the copyright owner, wish to exercise in the future. If you, as the copyright owner, desire to continue to exercise the same rights that are to be granting to a third party, make sure that the license you grant is nonexclusive.

- Place clear limits on any licenses or permissions granted to third parties, such as limits on quantity, time, purpose, geographic territory, market, method of distribution, type of display, etc.

- Do not grant greater or broader rights than necessary.

- Do not grant licenses to multiple parties that conflict with each other. For example, do not grant exclusive, unlimited rights to reproduce your copyrighted work to more than one person.

- To prevent a licensee from assigning rights in your copyrighted work to a third party, make sure the license is nontransferable.

Suggested Permission or Licensing Forms

The forms set forth on the following pages are intended to serve as guidelines to address issues that commonly arise within the quilting trade. These forms are not appropriate for all situations and they may fail to address fact-specific issues that arise in individual cases. For that reason, use these forms with care and seek professional legal advice before executing licenses with third parties who may have a higher level of sophistication in the business or legal arena.

Photography Issues

A problem frequently encountered by quilters involves third parties that take photographs of quilt designs without the copyright owner's permission. If the photographer later publishes the photograph in a newspaper article which could then lead to further unauthorized copying of that design, and the effect of that publication is to deny the copyright owner fees for the purchase of quilt designs, then such use is unlikely to fall under the privilege of fair use.

When displaying your original quilt designs at a trade show or in any public setting, in addition to ensuring that such work displays a copyright notice, display the following notice on your table or booth in a visible location:

THE QUILT DESIGNS DISPLAYED AT THIS BOOTH ARE PROTECTED BY COPYRIGHT. NO PHOTOGRAPHS OF THE DISPLAYED QUILT DESIGNS MAY BE TAKEN, DISTRIBUTED OR USED TO REPRODUCE THESE PROTECTED DESIGNS WITHOUT THE COPYRIGHT OWNER'S PRIOR WRITTEN PERMISSION.

If a photographer requests permission to photograph your quilt design for a limited purpose, a written form of permission should be completed and signed by both the copyright owner and the photographer. For example, if Linda Hahn were to grant a photographer the right to photograph her "Celestial" quilt design, the following form of permission could be used:

Linda Hahn (hereinafter "Copyright Owner") hereby grants permission to John Smith ("Photographer") with an address of 123 Main Street, Quiltersville, NJ 12321, to take photographs of the Celestial quilt pattern for the following limited purpose:

> *To include a single photograph of such quilt design in a newspaper article to be published by the Princeton Packet.*

This permission is being granted to Photographer on a royalty-free, nonexclusive, nontransferable basis, provided that the Photographer accepts the following additional terms:

> *(1)   The article must state that the quilt design is the copyrighted work of Copyright Owner and advise readers that permission to reproduce such design must be obtained from the Copyright Owner;*
>
> *(2)   The Photographer will obtain additional further permission from the Copyright Owner in order to publish such photograph in any other newspapers or publications;*
>
> *(3)   The Photographer will provide a copy of the published article to the Copyright Owner within one week of its publication.*

Signed:

_____

_____

Linda Hahn, Copyright Owner   John Smith, Photographer

Dated: _____

Dated: _____

Quilt Designs Sold to a Retailer for Distribution

If a quilt designer were to desire to sell a license to a retailer that will allow the retailer to copy her quilt designs and resell them to customers, the license should be in writing and should specify, at a minimum, terms concerning the license fee, the term of the license, and the number of copies permitted to be made for resale. Also, to maximize the copyright owner's rights to grant similar licenses to other retailers, the license should be nonexclusive. To prevent the retailer from assigning its rights to another party, the license should be nontransferable.

For example, if Merry May agreed to allow The Quilter's Kingdom, Inc., a local retailer, to make and distribute a limited number of copies of her Classic Holiday design, the following form of license agreement could be used:

License Agreement

*This License Agreement, dated as of January 1, 2009 (this "**License Agreement**"), is entered by and between Merry May, with an address of 1000 Quilters Way, Quiltersville, NJ 1232 ("**Licensor**") and The Quilter's Kingdom, Inc., a New Jersey corporation, with an address of 123 Main Street, Quiltersville, NJ 12321 ("**Licensee**").*

*WHEREAS, Licensee desires a license to copy and make a limited distribution of Licensor's copyrighted Classic Holiday quilt design (the "**Copyrighted Design**") and, subject to the terms stated*

in this License Agreement, Licensor has agreed to grant such license.

For good and valuable consideration, the receipt and sufficiency of which is hereby acknowledged, the Licensor and Licensee agree to be bound by the following terms and conditions:

1. Commencing as of the date hereof, Licensor hereby grants to Licensee a nontransferable, nonexclusive license to make not more than one hundred (100) copies of the Copyrighted Design for the sole purpose of selling such copies to its customers for private use. In exchange for such License, Licensee agrees to pay Licensor a license fee of Five Hundred Dollars ($500.00).

2. All copies of the Copyrighted Design shall bear the copyright notice of the Licensor as it appears on the original form provided to Licensee by Licensor. In addition, each package shall contain the following legend:

> *This quilt design is copyrighted by Merry May and may be used only by the purchaser for the noncommercial purpose of creating no more than three quilts for personal use. This quilt design may not be reproduced or distributed by the purchaser to other parties without the permission of the copyright owner.*

3. In the event that Licensee breaches any term of this License Agreement, Licensor shall have the right to terminate this License Agreement by providing written notice of termination to Licensee. In such event, Licensee shall not be entitled to a refund of any portion of the license fee. In addition, Licensor shall have the right to seek any and all legal and equitable remedies available under the law to protect Licensor's rights in the Copyrighted Design and under this License Agreement.

4. This License Agreement, and the rights granted to Licensee hereunder, may not be transferred or assigned by Licensee without the Licensor's prior written consent.

5. The terms and conditions of this License Agreement may not be amended or supplemented, except in a written form signed by both parties.

6. This License Agreement shall be governed by the laws of the State of New Jersey.

Agreed and Accepted: *Agreed and Accepted:*

 The Quilter's Kingdom, Inc.

 By: _____

_____

Merry May *Georgia Jones, President*

Instructional Materials

Whenever original instructional materials are to be distributed by the copyright owner that authored those materials, the copyright notice of the author should appear on each copy. Furthermore, to avoid the unauthorized copying and distribution by the students to third parties, it might be wise to include the following legend on the first page of your materials:

> *These instructional materials are protected by copyright and are distributed to students for their private use. These materials may not be copied and distributed to third parties without the prior written permission of the copyright owner.*

As a corollary piece of advice to quilters who prepare instructional materials, be sure to obtain permission before incorporating the copyrighted materials of others in your materials.

Conclusion

The primary purpose of this chapter is to provide the reader with a basic understanding of copyright law under the Copyright Act, as applied to the quilting art and trade. The benefits that can be derived from that improved understanding are two-fold: first, to provide practical guidance to quilters on how to protect their rights in original quilt designs and original instructional materials, and secondly, to help quilters avoid infringements of the copyrights of others. By taking some simple steps to protect your copyrights in your original designs and instructional materials, you can put more effort into the more important work of quilting—the art itself!

Disclaimer

This chapter on copyright is intended to provide helpful guidance to quilt designers, quilting instructors and others who make quilting either their business or their pleasure, or both. This chapter is not intended to serve as, and should not be relied upon by any individual or organization, as legal advice. The information in this chapter is of a general nature, may be subject to change (in particular, as the law changes), and is not a substitute for obtaining the advice of competent legal counsel.

Conclusion
by Merry May

When I first began teaching quilting classes, it was because of the generosity of my first quilting teacher, Peggy Della Porta, who called and asked if I was interested in taking over teaching at the local adult community education program. I questioned my ability and qualifications to teach because I still considered myself to be a beginner (despite quilting for almost ten years at that point). I said to Peggy (about teaching Basic Quilting), "But what if I do something wrong?" To which Peggy replied, "They're beginners – they won't know!"

Once I discovered the amount of preparation that went into designing projects, writing lesson plans and handouts, and being confronted by another experienced quilter who thought she was more qualified to teach (and repeatedly took my classes just to challenge me), I decided I needed some help.

I ordered and devoured the book, "Teaching Basic Quiltmaking" from the National Quilting Association. I followed the recommendations for the lessons, and immediately became more confident in my teaching abilities.

> **There is no better way of showing your support to someone than by offering a referral to that person within the same industry.**

A few months later I saw a classified ad in a quilting magazine promoting an exhibit by a group called the Tri-State Quiltmaking Teachers. At the time, I was not able to attend the exhibit, but the ad included a contact telephone number. I called to ask if new members were allowed to join, and what the requirements were. I was told where and when the next meeting was, so I worked up some courage and went.

It was a somewhat small group, perhaps a dozen people, but I was warmly welcomed by Judy Wolfrom, one of the members. Judy was kind enough to take me under her wing during the meeting, explaining different things to me, and encouraging me despite the fact that some of the "high rollers" in the quilting world were there. It turned out that

Patricia Morris (the author of the book, "Teaching Basic Quiltmaking") and Jeannette Muir were not only there, but were among those who had helped establish the group some time ago.

Over the years, Jeannette and Pat not only provided encouragement, but also gave me referrals for teaching and lecturing at quilt guilds throughout the area. There is no better way of showing your support to someone than by offering a referral to that person within the same industry.

A few years later they collaborated on an invitational quilt exhibit entitled, "Back to School." They had about fifty quilters who each chose a school topic and made small quilts of the same size. (My topic was Architecture.) The exhibit was first displayed at the Museum of the American Quilters' Society in Paducah, Kentucky; it then traveled to the Paley Design Center in Philadelphia, and then was shown a second time at the museum in Kentucky. In addition, the American Quilters' Society's magazine included an article about the exhibit, and I was honored to be one of only a handful of contributors whose entry was shown in the article.

Jeannette and Pat also invited me to take part in their book, "Heirloom Quilts from Old Tops," published by Krause. Each of the participants chose one of Jeannette's antique quilts as a jumping off point to make a new quilt based on the original quilt. As a result, my quilt "Turning Point" was included in their book.

In 1994 I invented a new product ("Gridded Geese"), and decided to take the plunge into vending at Quilt Market. The first Market I signed up for was in the spring of 1995, and it was located in Charlotte, North Carolina. In many ways it ended up being the "trip from hell" because so many things went wrong (starting with a broken-down, borrowed van on the day of the Oklahoma City bombing). But one thing which, at the

time was a "downer," ended up being the motivation for what I do now: encourage and coach others within the industry.

After we had set up our booth, the ladies who accompanied me went along to visit a local quilt shop. I overheard another customer talking with one of the shop's employees. They were talking about Quilt Market, and the customer mentioned that she was an exhibitor. I mentioned that I, too, was an exhibitor, and also a first-time exhibitor at Market. I then politely asked the other vendor a question about one of the Quilt Market events we had signed up for, but were not familiar with how it was organized. The woman's reply? "This is all trial by fire. Figure it out for yourself."

Once I picked my jaw up off of the floor, I decided that things did not need to be this way for anyone who had the guts to try something new within the quilting industry. So from that day on, I committed myself to encouraging others and offering a helping hand whenever I was asked.

Some of the people who received the benefit of my hard-earned knowledge have been wonderful, have kept in touch, and have even reciprocated over the years, teaching me about things they specialize in. Others barely thanked me. But that's not why I do this. In many ways this is how I "pay it forward" in honor of the generosity of people like Peggy Della Porta, Jeannette Muir, Judy Wolfrom, and the late Patricia Morris.

It is why Linda and I wrote this book.

So all I ask of any of you is to "pass it on" to others, especially if they ask for a bit of advice or if you think they deserve a word or two of encouragement. You never know when or how it will come back to reward you. I can tell you from my own experience, however, that it ultimately comes back to reward you tenfold or more. This is what I call "throwing it out to the universe to see where it will land."

Chapter Sixteen

Forms

Merry May

Professional Appraiser   •   Quiltmaker   •   Instructor

P.O. Box 305, Tuckahoe, NJ   08250-0305   USA

(609) 628-2231   ✸   FAX: (609) 628-3048   ✸   TwoTonsOfButtons@gmail.com

This is a complete appraisal report prepared <u>for client use only</u>.

Purpose of Appraisal: **(Ins./FMV)**
Name of Owner:
Address:
City/State/Zip:
Phone(s):

<u>**Description of Quilt:**</u>
Pattern Name/Title:

Dimensions: _____ Wide by _____Long (high)
Date Made: Documented: ___   Inferred: ___
Made By: Documented: ___   Inferred: ___

Construction Techniques used:

Fabrics used on exterior of quilt:

Batting:

Quilting Design:

Binding:

<u>**Workmanship:**</u>		
Construction:	**Quilting:**	**Condition/Restoration:**

Overall Condition of this Quilt:

   Excellent _____   Very Good _____   Good _____   Fair _____   Poor _____

<u>**Provenance/History of Quilt:**</u>

〜〜〜〜〜〜〜〜〜〜〜〜〜〜〜〜〜〜〜〜〜〜〜〜〜〜〜〜〜〜

Appraisal Value as of Today: $_____   **Appraisal Fee Paid:** $_____
Definition of Above Appraised Value: Ins. Replacement   OR   Fair Market Value
Appraisal Conducted by: _____
Date: _____   *See attached for Qualifications of Appraiser*

Quilt Appraisals by Merry May

Merry May is an experienced and recognized quilt appraiser from Tuckahoe, NJ. Appointments take about 30 minutes per item. The appraisal fee is $30.00 per item. A confidential written appraisal is completed for each quilt and one or more photos are taken for identification. **The completed appraisal and photo(s) will be mailed to you within one week.** Payment is due and payable to Merry May upon completion of the appraisal appointment.

Qualifications:
– Collector of antique quilts since 1983.
– Member of American Quilt Study Group since 1988; Regional Coordinator since its inception.
– Began lecturing on quilt history in 1990.
– Continued studying quilt history and values of antique quilts through extensive travel, reading research books and articles, and networking.
– Successfully completed Appraisal Certification Courses through the American Quilters' Society in July 2004 at the Vermont Quilt Festival.
– Has done verbal appraisals for South Shore Stitchers' Quilt Shows, as well as for Keystone Quilters (PA), Garden Patch Quilters (Millville, NJ), and Cape May County Historical & Genealogical Society.
– Guest Curator of the "Out of the Trunk" exhibit at the Cape May County Historical Museum, Cape May Court House, NJ from Sept. through Dec. 2005. Exhibit showcased thirty quilts from the Museum's collection.

Merry May - PO Box 305 - Tuckahoe, NJ 08250
· (609) 628-2231 · twotonsofbuttons@gmail.com ·

Easy Curved Piecing

Linda J. Hahn, NQACT
Lawnquilt@aol.com
www.twocountryquilters.com

Curved piecing has never been so easy using Linda's no agonizing method. Linda provides a handout which shows many different design options. Linda will also share her unique method of auditioning quilting designs. Linda will bring several variations of this quilt to class.

Supplies:

Template:	Elisa's Backporch 7" Template set (required)
Machine:	Cleaned, oiled and with a new needle. Extension cord. 1/4" foot
Cutting:	Rotary cutter (small one works better), mat & small square
Thread:	Neutral color cotton/cotton-covered for top – wind in bobbin also
Fabrics:	At least 36 10" squares (include lights and darks to mix and match). Please review attached handout of design possibilities for use in choosing your colors.
Other Stuff:	Cheap page protector Dry erase marker

Sample was made by Linda and Sarah Hahn. Long Arm quilted by Linda Hahn of Two Country Quilters using King Tut variegated cotton thread and Quilters Dream 70/30 batting. Binding applied by Rebecca Szabo.

CLASS CANCELLATION POLICY: Refunds of class fees will only be issued one week prior to class start, sorry NO exceptions! Please call the shop if you are unable to attend class.

Schoolhouse Enterprises	PO Box 305 Tuckahoe, NJ 08250-0305	tel 609.628.2256
		fax 609.628.3048
Merry May, Quiltmaker	www.MerryMayhem.com	Twotonsofbuttons@gmail.com

Commission Project Proposal

Prepared for: **Date Presented:**
Address:
Phone(s):
Email:

We hereby submit specifications and estimates for:

We Propose hereby to furnish material and labor - complete in accordance with above specifications, for the sum of: $_____.

All material is guaranteed to be as specified. All work to be completed in a workmanlike manner according to standard practices. Any alteration or deviation from above specifications involving extra costs will be executed only upon written orders, and will become an extra charge over and above the estimate. All agreements contingent upon delays beyond our control.

Authorized Signature by **Merry May:**

_____

Note: This Proposal may be withdrawn by us if not accepted within 30 days.

Terms: One-third (⅓) of the estimated fee is due upon placing your order; another one-third is due upon completion of the quilt top with your approval; final balance is due upon delivery. All major credit cards are welcome.

Acceptance of Proposal - The above prices, specifications and conditions are satisfactory and are hereby accepted. You are authorized to do the work as specified. Payment will be made as outlined above.

Date of Acceptance: _____ Signature: _____

Signature: _____

EXPENSE SHEET
Country Quilters Guild of Your Town, NY

Lecture: Margarita Madness $225.00
Workshop: New York Beauty $300.00

Mileage :

114 miles x 2 = 228 $0.505 per mile $115.14

Tolls:

Subtotal: $_____

Meals: (Receipts attached) $_____

TOTAL DUE: $_____

Please make check payable to Linda J. Hahn.

Thank you for inviting us to your guild. If you were pleased with our presentation, please tell other guilds - referrals are a large part of our business. If you were not, please tell us.

Two Country Quilters
24 Eliot Road
Manalapan, New Jersey 07726
(732) 792-1187
Lawnquilt@aol.com
www.twocountryquilters.com

TWO COUNTRY QUILTERS
24 Eliot Road
Manalapan, New Jersey 07726
(732) 792-1187
Lawnquilt@aol.com

LONG ARM MACHINE QUILTING WORK ORDER

Date accepted:_____   Date needed:_____ MQBM#_____
Name _____ Phone _____
Street address_____
E-mail _____
Who may we thank for the referral?_____

Describe your quilt top (color, pattern, approx. size, etc). Please also describe your back just in case they are separated.

Quilting pattern: _____   **Thread:** _____

Batting:

Customer provided (Type and size) _____
Purchase from Two Country Quilters: (circle one)
Hobbs 80/20   Quilters Dream Select   Quilters Dream Request   Quilters Dream 70/30
Special order (cost) _____

Backing: (Please mark center top on the back and top so we know how to load quilt)
Already prepared _____   Seaming required_____ ($10 first seam, $5.00 each addtl)

Binding:
$0.25 per inch (includes trimming quilt, preparing & attaching binding by machine, hand stitching to back)
To be done by customer _____   Use backing fabric _____   Binding fabric supplied _____

Modified Binding:
Fabric provided _____   Use backing fabric _____

Hanging Sleeve:
$0.30per inch (includes hemming, attaching to quilt and hand stitching down)
8 1/2" x width of quilt strip of fabric provided _____   Use backing fabric _____

TWO COUNTRY QUILTERS
24 Eliot Road
Manalapan, New Jersey 07726
(732) 792-1187
www.twocountryquilters.com

PREPARING YOUR QUILT FOR LONG ARM QUILTING
Answers to Frequently Asked Questions

We would like to return the best quilt possible to you at a reasonable price.
In order to do so, we ask that you please read this information sheet carefully.

MARK THE TOP, BACKING AND BATTING (if provided by you) with a safety pin along the top edge of your pieces. **This is so we know which sides match with which, and how to load the quilt. If not done, this takes time to measure each piece.**

BACKING AND BATTING (if provided by you) needs to be 4"-6" larger than the top.
This is to insure that there is plenty of fabric to load the quilt properly and get the proper tension on each side. Quilts, especially those with a lot of seams, may stretch during the quilting process. This is VERY important.

"BUSY" backs are highly recommended. **Busy backs hide stitch imperfections, stops and starts. Solid backs, depending on the quality of the fabric used, may experience bearding.**

PIECED BACKS SHOULD BE PIECED WITH A ½" VERTICAL SEAM WITH THE SEAM PRESSED OPEN. **This allows for the "stretchy" part to be loaded horizontally. If the back is pieced horizontally, there is no guarantee that the seam will be located in the center of the quilt. Additionally, if the backing is pieced off grain, there is a potential for the back seam to "wave" on the back. Selvedge edges MUST be removed.**

PROVIDING YOUR OWN BATTING DOES NOT NECESSARILY SAVE YOU MONEY.
We know what batting works best with our machine. If you provide your own batting, it MUST be marked (as above) and labeled with your name. If your batting is not cut large enough, we will substitute our batting and return yours. We offer several different types of battings at reasonable prices.

WE PREFER TO USE OUR THREAD. **We know which threads our machine likes.**
If we use your thread and run out at 4am, we cannot take your quilt off the frame to wait for you to provide us with another thread. We are basically out of business until we receive your thread and finish your quilt. For these reasons, we prefer to use our thread.

EDGES OF TOP AND BACK MUST BE TRIMMED STRAIGHT. **We need straight edges to properly load your quilt top and back onto the frame. Please take the time and trim all your edges straight. If we must take the time to straighten your edges, we must charge you for this service at $5.00 per edge.**

WHITE OR LIGHT COLORED QUILTS. **Please give special attention to the wrong side of your quilt top on light or white tops. Frayed seams/fabrics and piecing threads must be clipped otherwise there may be thread shadowing through the top. If we must take the time to clip these threads, you will be charged $25 per hour.**

-continued on reverse-

IN GENERAL. There are many factors which will effect the outcome of your quilt. We're going to cover some of the more important ones here.

1.   Batik fabric has a very high thread count (approx 200) while regular quilting cotton is approx 78 – this creates an imbalance and could effect the tension and stitches. We recommend if you have a batik on top, a cotton on the bottom will give you a nicer result.

2.   If you have any bias edges on your top, please stitch around the outside edge to stabilize your quilt, otherwise it will stretch when on the frame. If we do this for you, there is a charge of $25 per hour.

3.   It is the customer's responsibility to be sure all seams are tight before sending it to us. If seams come apart during the quilting process, we cannot take the quilt off the frame – the seam must be top stitched.

4.   Please let us know ahead of time if there are any "problems" with your quilt, such as a wavy border, "B" cup in a block. If we know ahead of time we can work with it and try to make adjustments.

5.   DO NOT embellish your quilt until the quilting is completed.

6.   If your quilt top is not straight and square when you bring it to us, you will not receive a square quilt back. Please be sure that you measure your borders before applying them to the quilt. If you don't -your quilt will be distorted. Please contact us for an instruction sheet on how to properly apply borders.

7.   For the best tension, fabrics on the top and back should be the same weight and quality throughout the quilt.

8.   Any extra work that we must do in order to prepare your quilt for quilting is billed at $25 per hour.

CUSTOM SHOW QUILTS – **Show quality quilts start at $0.04 cents per square inch. These quilts take much longer to do. They are priced according to the density, design and amount of quilting requested.**

ENTERING SHOWS. **If you enter your quilt in a show, please give us the appropriate credit for the quilting. Usually your work order will indicate which one of us quilted your piece. We'd also love to have a photo of you, your ribbon and quilt for our website. We will give you a $5.00 gift certificate if you e-mail us the .jpeg photo of your quilt (and permission to use it on our website and in our Power-Point presentation).**

EXTRA CHARGES - **There is a $25 charge if we must "turn" the quilt to properly quilt the border design. To turn the quilt, we must unload the quilt, turn it and then re-load the quilt. This can take anywhere from 45 minutes to an hour. If you request that we change thread colors on your quilt, there is a thread change charge of $5.00 in addition to the thread charge. This is because it takes extra time to re-thread and check the tension settings for each thread.**

BINDING – **If we are doing the binding (either modified or full) we prefer to cut and prepare the binding ourselves. This insures that we have the right size and amount needed.**

The Lights on Broadway
36" x 36"

Linda J. Hahn
24 Eliot Road
Manalapan, New Jersey 07726
(732) 792-1187
lawnquilt@aol.com

Top pieced by	Linda J. Hahn & Barbara E. Smith
Long Arm Machine Quilted by	Linda J. Hahn – Two Country Quilters
Machine Used	Gammill Classic Plus
Quilting pattern	Custom Freehand
Batting	Quilters Dream Request
Thread	Superior Metallic - Purple
Pattern	New York Beauty by Linda J. Hahn
Year Completed	2008
Shows Entered:	2008 New Jersey Quilt Convention

Story Card:

New York beauty blocks pieced by Linda J. Hahn and Barbara E. Smith. Custom Freehand quilted by Linda J. Hahn of Two Country Quilters in Superior Metallic thread. Made as a sample for my Machine Quilting and New York Beauty workshops.

#2 in a series of New York Beauty quilts. Made with accumulated batik scraps

TWO COUNTRY QUILTERS
Business Plan

Linda J. Hahn
24 Eliot Road
Manalapan, New Jersey 07726
www.twocountryquilters.com
(732) 792-1187

Date: October 26, 2008

Description of the Business

My business encompasses several areas of the quilting industry.

- Long Arm Machine Quilting
- Teaching at local quilt shop and at guilds/quilt shows
- Vending hard to find and specialty quilting items at area quilt shows
- Designing quilts for Elizabeth's Studio, LLC
- Book Author
- Offering quilt cruises and getaways under Double Trouble Studios

Target Market and Customers

- Long Arm - quilters in the NJ area
- Teaching - quilt guilds and shows along East Coast of U.S.
- Vending - local guild shows
- Book author - professional and non-professional quilters

Growth In This Business

At the time this Plan is being written the United States is suffering from a recession. Quilters are more conscious of their purchases and are not splurging on special items. Long Arm customers are choosing to apply their own bindings as opposed to using our service.

Pricing Structure

See attached long arm quilting brochure for long arm quilting prices.
See attached teaching brochure for lecture and workshop pricing.

Credentials and Professional Experience

See attached professional resume.

Structure of the Business

Two Country Quilters is operated as a sole proprietorship by Linda J. Hahn.

Professional Consultants

Bank	Sovereign Bank, Englishtown, New Jersey
Attorney	Vincent E. Halleran, Jr., Freehold, New Jersey
Accountant	Kevin Meszaros, Matawan, New Jersey

Financing Strategy

At the present time, the checking account balance is $_____. There are no outstanding debts on behalf of the business.

Attached is a list of projected expenses that the business will incur in 2009.

Attached is a list of projected income to the business in 2009.

Marketing, Advertising and Promotional Plans

In 2009, I plan to forward my teaching credentials to the following venues:

I will also have my long arm flyers re-printed for distribution to area quilt shops and quilt guilds.

Purchasing and Inventory Control

We are booked for several vending engagements in 2009 as follows:
    February 2009 - venue
    October 2009 - venue

Inventory was depleted at the end of 2008 and must be re-stocked prior to the first vending engagement. It is estimated that the cost to re-stock will be $___

An assessment needs to be done on the current inventory to determine what items may be reduced in price to encourage sales.

Analysis of Competition

At the present time, there are 2 other long arm quilters in my area. A comparison of their businesses to this business is as follows:

Competitor vending booths vary from show to show, area to area. The constant can be construed to be the area quilt shops who also participate as vendors. Our booth can remain competitive by offering a variety of merchandise not carried in quilt shops.

Growth Strategy

Long Arm Quilting - I hope to secure more custom quilting jobs and to improve my skills. In order to do this, I will (do the following)

Teaching - I plan to forward my teaching resume to the aforementioned venues. I would also like to develop another lecture and workshop to add to my current offerings.

Schoolhouse Enterprises	PO Box 305 Tuckahoe, NJ 08250-0305	tel 609.628.2256
		fax 609.628.3048
Merry May	www.MerryMayhem.com	Twotonsofbuttons@gmail.com

Restoration Project Proposal

Prepared for: **Date Presented:**
Address:
Phone(s):
Email:
We hereby submit specifications and estimates for:

We Propose hereby to furnish material and labor - complete in accordance with above specifications, for the sum of: $_____.

All material is guaranteed to be as specified. All work to be completed in a workmanlike manner according to standard practices. Any alteration or deviation from above specifications involving extra costs will be executed only upon written orders, and will become an extra charge over and above the estimate. All agreements contingent upon delays beyond our control.

Authorized Signature by **Merry May:**

_____

Note: This Proposal may be withdrawn by us if not accepted within 30 days.

Terms: One-third (⅓) of the estimated fee is due upon placing your order; final balance is due upon delivery. All major credit cards are welcome.

Acceptance of Proposal - The above prices, specifications and conditions are satisfactory and are hereby accepted. You are authorized to do the work as specified. Payment will be made as outlined above.

Date of Acceptance: _____   Signature: _____

                                                                    Signature: _____

Merry May

• Quiltmaker • Designer • Instructor • Innovator • Appraiser

P.O. Box 305, Tuckahoe, NJ   08250-0305 USA

(609) 628-2231 ✻ www.MerryMayhem.com ✻ TwoTonsOfButtons@gmail.com

RESUME   06/08

Education: Associates Degree, Art, Southwestern College, San Diego, CA, 1977; Continued education in quilting industry by attending workshops and/or seminars several times each year; continues to study and research quilt history. Took the AQS "Appraisal Certification" classes at Vermont Quilt Festival in 2004.

Quilt-Related Work Experience: Began making quilted pillows in 1973 (self-taught); first full-size quilt completed in 1984. Teacher of Basic Quiltmaking (adult Ed) 1988 to present. Also teaches various workshops throughout the Eastern Coast of the US. Lectures on "History of American Quilting" from 1990 to present; includes presentations to numerous local organizations, historical societies, and schools. Does quilt history consulting (incl. "Antique Quiltathon" sessions - verbal appraisals of antique quilts). Does small-scale quilt commissions. Designs original quilt patterns, including a popular series of mystery quilts under the pen name of "Merry Mayhem's Mystery Quilts." Invented and copyrighted the "Gridded Geese" system to mass-produce Flying Geese units, 1994. Works part-time at Calico 'n Cotton, a quilt shop in Ocean City, NJ; since 1999. Faculty member of Quilt University (www.QuiltUniversity.com) from 2000 to 2004; Vermont Quilt Festival instructor, 2002, 2003, 2006 & 2008; NJ Quilt Convention instructor, June 2003, 2006; NJ All Star in 2008. Taught for Brother International on two occasions in 2003. Guest curator of quilt exhibit ("Out of the Trunk") at the Cape May County Historical Museum, Sept.'05-Apr. 2006. Marketing Consultant for Elizabeth's Studio, 2007 to present. Partners with Linda Hahn in establishing Double Trouble Studios, 2008.

Quilt-Related Memberships and Activities: American Quilter's Society, 1986 to present; American Quilt Study Group, 1990 to present; Regional Coordinator for AQSG in Southern N.J., 1992 to present; National Quilting Association, 1986 to present; South Shore Stitchers (local guild), 1986 to present, Treasurer 1991 to 1993, served on Quilt Show Committee during all guild shows, Co-Chairman of 1993, 2003 & 2005 Quilt Shows, Vice President, 1994, President 1995, Program chair 1997/98; Tri-State Quiltmaking Teachers (now Quilt Professionals' Network) 1990 to present, Treas. for 1992-93, '96-97, and '99-2003 terms, Pres. for 1994-95 term; State Quilt Guild of NJ, founding member 1997, guild Treasurer & Newsletter Editor 1997-99 & 2001-04, Pres. 2005-07; member of original Board of Directors, Riverfront Renaissance Center for the Arts (Millville, NJ), July 1999 to Jan. 2000. Leads "Gilda' Quilter's" at Gilda's Club South Jersey in Somers Point, NJ - Apr. 2002 to present.

Awards and Recognitions: Nominated for Professional Quilter magazine's "Teacher of the Year" in 2003 and 2008. Taped a segment about collecting antique quilts on PAX Network's show Treasures in Your Home, Jan. 2000; aired 1/28/2000. Interviewed in "Quiltmaker Tales" video special; taped by NJN during the State Quilt Guild of NJ's first statewide quilt show, Nov. '99; "Thanks for the Memories" quilt also featured; won a First Place ribbon for "Liberty" quilt. Viewer Tip appeared on Sewing with Nancy PBS program; Part 3 of the "Quilting Options" series, first aired in Fall 1991; also published in "501 Sewing Hints" by Nancy Zieman, published by Oxmoor House. Has won awards in quilt block contests, including: Quilter's Newsletter Magazine's 20th Anniversary Contest, 1989; 2nd Generation Sunbonnet Family Reunion block contest sponsored by Groves Publishing, 1990 (Bertha Corbett Award).

Publications: Numerous patterns, articles and photos published in magazines, including McCall's Quilting, McCall's Quick Quilting, Quiltworks Today, Traditional Quiltworks, Quilting Today, American Quilter, and Ladies' Circle Patchwork Quilts.

"Turning Point" included in the book: Heirloom Quilts from Old Tops; Krause Publications, 2001.

Sponsored Quilting Today magazine's Flying Geese Challenge, featured in Issue 75 (Oct. 1999); "Reds and Whites and Blues All Over!" quilt published in Issue 83.

Bi-monthly columnist for The Country Register of Del/NJ on Quilting, Dec. 1998 to April 2000.

Article, "The Value of Networking" in Summer 1996 issue of Professional Quilter magazine.

Was subject of a feature article in Issue 35 of Quilting Today magazine, April 1993.

Exhibits: Solo exhibit at Down Jersey Folklife Center, WheatonArts.org in Millville, NJ - Jan. 25 -Mar. 31, 2008.

"ArchiteXture" wall hanging included in "Back to School" invitational exhibit, first shown at the Museum of the American Quilter's Society, Paducah, KY, October 1999 through January 8, 2000; Paley Design Center, Phila., PA May -Aug. 2000; Museum of the American Quilter's Society, Paducah, KY again in April 2001. Down Jersey Folklife Center, Wheaton Village, Millville, NJ, December 1996; "East Point Lighthouse" quilt on permanent loan, June 1997 to present; also solo exhibit March/April 1998.

"Reflections in the Eye of a Needle", group exhibit, October-December 1994, Brian Parent Center, Millville, NJ.

"Primarily Pablo" jacket included in the 1992 Hoffman Challenge Clothing Collection traveling exhibit, October 1992 to December 1993.

Other Hobbies and Interests: Manages a local cemetery; owns and operates Schoolhouse Enterprises, a small, home-based mail order business; co-founder of Net@mity, LLC a web-based business; charter member of Greater Tuckahoe Area Merchants' Association, April 1995 to present, served as President, 1996 and 1999, Sec. 2006 to present; enjoys networking with other quilters, and mentoring to those who wish to join the professional quilting community; owns two tons of buttons (it seemed like a good idea at the time!).

Contract:
This contract is between Creative Sew & Sews, LLC located at 339 Route 9 South, Manalapan, NJ 07726 and the following:

Services:
Instructor of Fiber Arts education, classes are scheduled in advance to meet at the location stated above. Please consult current class schedule for specific times and dates.

Fees: Fees for instruction will be collected by Creative Sew & Sews LLC and instructors will be reimbursed by Creative Sew & Sews, LLC within five business days after course completion.
Reimbursement as follows:
1-3 students = $15 per instruction hour
4+ students = $25 per instruction hour

Additional Agreements & Conditions: Instructor will abide by employee conduct codes as outlined in store operations manual. Instructor will provide Creative Sew & Sews, LLC with a complete course description, current sample of product or project and a detailed supply list prior to the publication and distribution of quarterly newsletter. All instructors will receive a 15% discount on all regularly priced store merchandise during length of contract. Classes will be advertised via printed quarterly newsletter and the store's website, www.creativesewnsews.com.

We the undersigned, agree to all terms and conditions of this contract.

Date

Rebecca Szabo, Creative Sew & Sews LLC   Date

Merry May
• Quiltmaker • Designer • Instructor • Innovator
P.O. Box 305, Tuckahoe, NJ   08250-0305 USA
(609) 628-2256 ✻ FAX: (609) 628-3048 ✻ twotonsofbuttons@gmail.com

SPONSORING ORGANIZATION:
ADDRESS:
CITY/STATE/ZIP:

CONTACT PERSON: **TELEPHONE** OF CONTACT PERSON: (____)_____
                                            Cell: (____)_____

LECTURE/WORKSHOP to be Taught:

DATE(S) OF LECTURE/WORKSHOP:
TIME(S):

LOCATION OF CLASSES:

CLASS SIZE: _____Minimum   _____Maximum

TRAVEL EXPENSES
Your Choice:
_____ Current IRs mileage rate plus tolls, plus food and lodging,
                        OR
_____ Round-trip coach airfare plus ground transportation, plus UPS shipping and insurance charges for round-trip transport of quilts (for History lecture only). Sponsoring Organization arranges for air and ground transportation. Food and lodging will also be provided for the duration of travel and teaching period as contracted by Sponsoring Organization. Name and telephone number of person making travel arrangements:

_____

FEES & REIMBURSEMENTS:
Lecture: $275.00 plus travel (see below)
Half-Day Workshop: $275.00 plus travel
One-Day Workshop: $450.00 plus travel
Two-Day Workshop: $800.00 plus travel

LODGING OPTIONS:
_____ Motel/Hotel or Bed & Breakfast in area; Sponsoring Organization makes reservation. Name and telephone number of person making room reservation:

_____

CANCELLATIONS:
• In the event of insufficient enrollment for a workshop, one week's cancellation notice is required.
• Otherwise, no less than 48 hours notice is required, except in cases of extreme weather conditions, severe illness, or acts of God which are beyond our control. Sponsoring Organization is only responsible for any transportation costs which are not refundable.

We hereby accept the above terms and conditions as set forth in this contract.

Sponsoring Organization, by_____Date_____

Merry May_____Date_____

Room Set-up Needed for this Lecture:
One or two tables for presentation plus sale of product, if applicable.
Some floor space adjacent to the presentation table for displaying quilts.

Linda J. Hahn
24 Eliot Road
Manalapan, New Jersey 07726
Phone: 732-792-1187 – Cell Phone 732-610-1116
E-mail: Lawnquilt@aol.com
website: www.twocountryquilters.com

LETTER OF AGREEMENT/CONTRACT FOR WORKSHOPS & LECTURES

This is to confirm our verbal agreement that Linda J. Hahn will present the following workshop(s) and/or lecture(s) for:

Conference/Guild Name _____

Address _____

Phone _____ Fax _____ E-mail _____

to be held on date(s) _____ _____

Fees: (as of 1/1/09)
Lecture $275.00
Workshop $400.00 (whole day 6 hrs incl. lunch) $200.00 (half day - 3 hrs.)

*$20 per person additional for workshops over 20 people – max. 25 people.

Expenses:
Round trip millage @ prevailing IRS rate   Photocopying $0.02 per page
Round trip highway tolls   Meals ($35 per teaching day/$17 travel day)
Accommodations (if venue over 2 hours driving time from my home)

Extra days:
If Linda needs to spend extra time at your location in order to save the guild(s) money, or to share Linda with other guilds, the guild(s) will be responsible for all expenses on these extra days. From time to time, Linda may travel with her husband or daughter. Guild is not responsible for their expenses. In case of hotels that have an extra charge for a second person in the room, Linda will pay the extra charge.

Lodging/Meals
Linda is up and moving (and needing coffee!) at 4 am, so she would prefer to stay in a bed & breakfast or hotel with a room on the first floor with wireless internet access. Meals should be available at the hotel or close by. Unless otherwise agreed, there will be a $35 per diem meal allowance (which covers breakfast, lunch and dinner) per teaching day or $17 per half day (covering b'fast/lunch or dinner).

Sales:
Two Country Quilters are available to vend hard to find and specialty supplies & gifts at the lecture/workshop venue. The guild/conference will not expect to collect any commission on these sales. Linda will not take teaching time to promote any products. The guild may choose to provide a teacher angel to assist Linda.

Vending permitted? _____ At Lecture _____ At Workshop

CANCELLATION POLICY: If the guild cancels within 15 days of the scheduled date, guild shall be responsible for payment of $100.00 within ten days of cancellation.

TITLE OF LECTURE/WORKSHOP _____ _____

DATE_____TIME_____

LOCATION (please include street address and phone number for GPS)

_____

TITLE OF LECTURE/WORKSHOP _____

DATE_____ TIME _____

LOCATION (please include street address and phone number for GPS)

_____

A signed copy of this letter of understanding must be returned before a firm commitment can be made.

The Guild/Conference will provide the name of a second person in your organization who can be contacted in the event that the organizer/program chair is not available.

I have read the above letter of agreement and I understand and agree to its terms.

GUILD REPRESENTATIVE

Name (print) _____

Address _____

Phone _____Cell Phone _____

E-mail _____Fax _____

Signature _____

Second person in your group who can be contacted:

Name (print) _____

Address _____

Phone _____Cell Phone _____

E-mail _____Fax _____

_____   _____
LINDA J. HAHN   DATE

2009 NJ QUILT CONVENTION
ENTRY INFORMATION

The State Quilt Guild of NJ, Inc. is proud to present the "Fancy This, Fancy That" NJ Quilt Convention June 11-13, 2009. This judged quilt competition will be displayed at the NJ Expo Center, Edison, NJ. NQA certified judges will evaluate all entries and award each first place winner $100.00 cash in ALL adult categories. Ribbons will be awarded in all categories for first, second, third and honorable mentions. In addition, cash prizes will be offered for various merit awards such as Best of Show, Best Machine Workmanship, Best Hand Workmanship, Best Use of Color, Best Longarm Quilting, Best Traditional Design, Best Innovative Design, Judge's Choice & The Melanie Normann Memorial Award. The Best Individual Youth entry will receive a sewing machine and all youth entries receive a participation ribbon. Please read the entry rules carefully as SQG of NJ, Inc. reserves the right to disqualify any entry not meeting these criteria.

- ALL entries MUST be clean, free of pins, pet hair and smoke.
- ALL entries MUST be constructed of fabric and quilted.
- ALL entries, with the exception of the "small" or "wearables" category, MUST have a 4" hanging sleeve SEWN on the back to be hung.
- ALL entries must have a label sewn to the lower left-hand corner of the back.
- ALL labels must be temporarily covered with basted-on fabric for the judging process. No freezer paper or pins please.
- Entries cannot contain a frame or hanging device or present problems in handling or shipping.
- Items must be made in 2005 or later and not entered in any previous SQG of NJ, Inc. show.
- Entry limit of 2 quilts per category, per person.

CATEGORIES

Traditional/ Pieced	Based on a well established or commonly known patterns. Pieced patchwork predominates over appliqué or other techniques in amount or effect. Made and quilted by 1 (same) person.
Innovative/ Art Quilt	Extending beyond traditional disciplines and exercising progressive independence and originality in theory, design, color or technique. Made and quilted by 1 (same) person.
Applique	Appliqué predominates over piecing or other technique in either amount or effect. Made and quilted by 1 (same) person.
Small	Any quilt with a total perimeter of less than 92", including miniatures. Made and quilted by 1 (same) person.
Group	Any quilt made by 2 or more people, regardless of size.
Duet	THIS IS A NEW CATEGORY. A quilt that is constructed by only one person and is only quilted by another person. The quilter may or may not be a professional.
Theme	Any quilt regardless of size that is your interpretation of the theme: Fancy This, Fancy That. Entries may be made by 1 or more person(s).
Individual Youth	Entrant must be between 7-15 years of age. Adult assistance is permitted in this category.
Group Youth	Entries made by two or more youths, with or without adult assistance. Example: Class quilt
Wearable	Must be garment(s). Accessories (purses, belts) can only accompany garments and cannot be entered alone.

HOW TO ENTER CHECKLIST

- Completed entry form, one for EACH entry. PLEASE PRINT! This form may be photocopied.
- Entry fee of $10.00 per entry, make checks payable to "SQG of NJ, Inc." You may write a single check if all entries that are sent in the same envelope.
- Sew on a 4" hanging sleeve on the back of each entry, except "small" quilts.
- Label each entry in the lower left-hand corner on the back and cover it temporarily for judging with basted fabric, no freezer paper or straight pins please.
- Mail entry forms no later than April 1, 2009 to: Jenny Quilter, PO Box 999, Any City, NJ 00000
- If return shipping is requested, a non-refundable fee of $15 per box must accompany entry form.Questions? Check our website at NJQUILTS.ORG or phone Geri at 888-888-8888
- See next page for drop-off and shipping instructions.

HAND DELIVERY INSTRUCTIONS

Hand delivery can be made at one of three convenient drop off locations and dates.

> Wed. 6/3/09, 4pm-8pm: Cozy Quilt Shoppe, 466 Kinderkamack Rd, River Edge.
>   Directions only: 201-483-3775 or www.cozyquilter.com
> Fri. 6/5/09, 10am-2pm: Quilting Possibilities, 512 Rt. 9 South, Forked River.
>   Directions only: 609-242-0033 or www.quiltingposs.com
> Sat. 6/6/09, 10am-2pm: Creative Sew & Sews, 30 Main St. , Englishtown
>   Directions only: 732-792-0083 or www.creativesewnsews.com

DO NOT drop off entries at these locations at any time other than the specified dates and times.
Questions regarding drop off? Phone Queenie at 888-888-8888

- Bring each entry in its own cloth pillowcase with your name and address clearly marked on the outside.
- Please do not roll or put quilts on cardboard tubes; they will be declined entry.
- We will verify at drop-off that quilts meet entry criteria and that they have a 4" hanging sleeve & that fabric covered labels are sewn on, thanks! A receipt for pickup will be issued. If you need the entry shipped back to you, please bring a shipping carton with you.

SHIPPING INSTRUCTIONS

Quilts should be shipped to: Queen Quilter, 123 Main Street, Other City, NJ 00001
and MUST arrive between June 2-June 6, 2009. (Judging starts on June 8)

- Place each entry in its own cloth pillowcase in a sturdy box. If you have more than one entry you may ship them in the same box, except for large quilts. Your entries will be returned in the same box via UPS. Make sure each pillowcase has your name and address on it.
- Include a self-addressed, stamped envelope, which will be used to mail your entry receipt.
- ONE ENTRANT per box, please **mark each entry with its title that matches your entry form**.
- **Do not use plastic bags, Styrofoam, pellets or tubes to pack items.**

INSTRUCTIONS TO PICK UP YOUR QUILT

You may pick up your entries at the NJ Expo Center on Sat. 6/13 starting at 5:30pm.
Entry receipts must be presented at time of pick up. Entries **must** be checked out by show staff.

INSTRUCTIONS TO HAVE YOUR QUILT SHIPPED BACK TO YOU

Make sure you have provided:

- A carton for return shipping if entry was dropped off.
- A self-addressed shipping label, NO PO Box addresses please.
- A non-refundable fee of $15.00 per box (payable to "SQG of NJ, Inc.") with your entry form.

VOLUNTEERING

The State Quilt Guild of NJ, Inc. is a non-profit, volunteer organization. We need YOUR help!
The following areas are in need of volunteers!

- ❖ Quilt Drop Off (6/3,6/5 & 6/6)
- ❖ Judging (6/8-6/10)
- ❖ Quilt Hanging (6/8-6/10)
- ❖ Hostess/White Glove (6/11-6/13)
- ❖ Admissions/Lobby (6/11-6/13)
- ❖ Workshop Registration Booth(6/11-6/13)
- ❖ Quilt Un-Hanging & Return (6/13)

All volunteers who are not registered workshop attendees, may choose to receive discounted admission to the exhibit hall. Please contact Queen Quilter at info@njquilts.org or phone 888-888-8888 to sign up today!

NJ QUILT CONVENTION ENTRY FORM This form may be photocopied.
PLEASE PRINT OR TYPE
Check here if you do not want your quilt judged _____
☐ **Postmark by April 1, 2009, ONE FORM PER ENTRY, $10.00 per entry**

Name(s) _____
(For group entry give a contact name with address and list names as you would like them to appear on reverse)

Street Address _____
(No PO Boxes for return shipping)

City _____ State _____ Zip _____

E-mail
Phone _____ (required for confirmation)

Title of Entry _____ Year Completed(2005-present) _____

Top Made By _____ Quilted By _____

Total Measurement all 4 sides _____ * Insurance Value _____ * Required
(Over $1000 bed, $500 others requires a written appraisal)
(If no $ amount is declared no insurance will be paid)

Method of Quilting: Hand____ Machine____ Longarm ____

Categories, check only one: Total all sides of quilt to determine size.

☐ Bed Quilt- Applique (280" or larger)
☐ Bed Quilt –Pieced (280" or larger)
☐ Wall Quilt- Applique (93"- 279")
☐ Wall Quilt- Pieced (93"- 191")
☐ Wall Quilt –Pieced (192"- 279")
☐ Innovative (93" or larger)
☐ Group
☐ Duet
☐ 2008 Theme (any size)
☐ Small Quilt (up to 92")
☐ Individual Youth (ages 7-15) Age:_____
☐ Group Youth (ages 7-15)
☐ Wearable Art

Please write a brief story (25 words or less) for the story cards, subject to editing: If a Theme entry tell us how you interpreted the theme in your quilt. Use another sheet if needed.

_____
_____
_____
_____
_____
_____
_____
_____
_____
_____

DELIVERY/RETURN INSTRUCTIONS
Delivery Method: Hand: _____ 6/3, 6/5 or 6/6 at various locales, see instructions
Shipped: _____ Must be received by 6/6, refer to shipping instructions
Return Method: Hand: _____ After 5:30pm on 6/13, bring entry receipt!
Shipped: _____ No PO boxes, please refer to return instructions, enclose $15 fee!

Signature: _____
I wish to enter the above quilted item and agree to abide by the rules and decisions of the judge and the SQG of NJ, Inc. I understand that the SQG of NJ, Inc. will take precautions to protect my entry but cannot be held responsible for events beyond its control. You have my permission to photograph this entry and use the photograph for event-related publicity and/or promotion both before and after the show, including our website NJQUILTS.org. All entrants must have written permission from the creators of the piece.

SEND FORM with fees TO: Jenny Quilter, PO Box 999, Any City, NJ 00000
Show Committee Use
Entry form rec'd _____ Category: _____ Total # of entries: _____
Entry Fee: _____ Return Shipping: _____ Total: _____ Ck# _____

NJ QUILT CONVENTION
June 11-13, 2009

New Jersey Convention & Expo Center
Edison, NJ

500+ Quilts & Wearables in a judged competition featuring cash prizes!

Full and Half Day Workshops with Helen Squire, Linda Cantrell, Anna Faustino, Cyndi Sauder, Lacey J. Hill & Nancy Tejo

Special Lecture Series & Reception

Luncheon/ Lecture with Helen Squire on Sat. 6/13

Merchant Mall with over 30 vendors

Special Exhibit Area including; NJ All-Star: Linda Hahn, WWII Collection, Antique Quilts, Goddess Project, Brownstone Quilters, NJ & Teacher's Row

Youth Interactive Area & Teen T-shirt Challenge

Free Lectures & Demos

Quilt Appraisals with Mary Kerr

Bus Trip Discounts

Raffle Tickets on sale for a Queen Sized Quilt,

Food Court

Presented by the State Quilt Guild of NJ, Inc.

Sponsored by: Quilting Possibilities/Elna, Pieceful Choices Quilt Shop, Bernina Sewing Center of Matawan, Pennington Quiltworks, P & B Fabrics, Creative Sew & Sews, The Village Quilter Kim Morris, Longaberger Consultant, Two Country Quilters, Sandra Dorrbecker, Bernice Pak, Pieceful Shores Quilt Guild & Geri Wolf of Threadmakers Mystery Quilt Getaways

Visit www. NJquilts.org for more info

BBQ Weekend Spring 2009

with Linda Hahn, Merry May and Sarah Hahn

FRIDAY, April 24 - Be sure to stop at Calico 'n Cotton in Ocean City on your way down. Don't forget to take your special discount coupon!! (Will be mailed to you.)
· 3 PM to 7 PM - Check-in at Adventurer Inn in in Wildwood Crest, NJ; set up sewing areas for classes in **7th Floor Convention Room**; Dinner on your own. Note: Rooms each have an apartment-sized refrigerator, microwave, coffee pot and small table & chairs.
· 7 to 7:30 PM - Welcome Reception with Wine & Cheese Party; **bring your favorite snack!**
· 7:30 to 8 PM - Introductions; Show 'n Tell of previous projects from BBQs.
· 8 PM to ??? - **"Quivial Pursuit" Game Show** with Merry May; Door Prizes will be awarded during the program. Continue visiting, setting up, and/or EATING!!
SATURDAY, April 25 - 7 to 9 AM - Breakfast in restaurant downstairs; gratuity <u>not</u> included ($1 per person suggested).
  9 AM to 12 Noon - Morning Session
  12 Noon to 1:30 PM - Lunch (on your own, or order out "Dutch Treat")
  1:30 to 4:30 PM - Afternoon Session
  4:45 to 6:15 PM - Dinner at a local restaurant (we provide; gratuity included)
SUNDAY, April 26 - 7 to 9 AM Breakfast in restaurant downstairs; gratuity <u>not</u> included.
  9 AM to 12 Noon - Morning Session
  12 Noon to 1:30 PM - Lunch (on your own, or order out "Dutch Treat")
  2:00 PM - Weekend ends; have a safe trip home!

<<<<<<<<<<<<<<<<*NEW SYSTEM!*>>>>>>>>>>>>>>>>>>>>

OUR PRICING:
  $130 per person, with <u>$75 Deposit per person</u> to be submitted with Registration. $25 of the Registration fee is non-refundable.

BALANCE DUE: MARCH 31. There is an additional $10 fee if your Balance is not paid before March 31.

ROOMS: Call the Adventurer Inn and make your own room reservation! (609) 522-0029 or (800) 232-7873 Be sure to mention that you are part of the QUILTERS group.

<u>Refund Policy:</u> 100% refund until March 31, less $25 non-refundable deposit; 75% refund from April 1 through April 15, less $25 non-refundable deposit.
· · · NO REFUNDS AFTER APRIL 15. · · · ·
Supply Lists will be sent once you have chosen your workshops, and your Deposit has been received. **Directions to the Adventurer Inn** will be sent about six weeks before the BBQ weekend.
**** There is a $30 fee for any returned checks ****

CLASS DESCRIPTIONS

FRIDAY EVENING PROGRAM:

"Quivial Pursuit" Game Show Hosted by a Famous Unknown Quilter
Trivia questions related to quiltmaking and quilt history. Contestants redeem point coupons for "fabulous" prizes!

<<<< TWO-DAY WORKSHOP:

"Hanafabuki" with Linda Hahn - Intermediate* ☀
Make this beautiful quilt top with Oriental fabrics and Linda's simplified instructions.

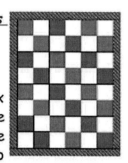

SATURDAY CLASS - The following Class is a One-Day Workshop: >>>>>

"Machine Quilt as You Go" with Merry May - Advanced Beginner & Up* ☀
You should be able to complete this 40" x 52" project in class (except for the binding) which was designed by the instructor so you can learn at least two ways of machine quilting your projects on your home sewing machine. Other options will be shown as well.

SUNDAY CLASS - The following Sunday Class is a Half-Day Workshop:

"3-D Attic Windows" with Merry May - Advanced Beginner & up* ☀
You won't believe how easy it is to make these Attic Windows blocks! The templates are even set up so you can easily fussy-cut the squares for inside the windows! We used the "Sock Monkeys at the Beach" fabrics from Moda for our sample, but you can use pretty much anything you want for your project!

* Please see the Insert about Skill Levels included in this mailing.

☀ = Pre-Order Books & Patterns for a special BBQ Discount!

INSTRUCTORS' BIOGRAPHIES

Linda J. Hahn, of Manalapan, NJ, started quilting in 1993 and teaching in 1994. Linda received her National Quilting Association Teacher Certification in 1998. She was nominated (2001, 2004 and 2008) for Professional Quilter magazine's Teacher of the Year Award. Linda has served as President, and served as conference co-chair for the Quilt Professionals' Network for several years. Linda taught on quilting cruises in 2004, 2005 and 2006, and taught in Bermuda on two occasions. She has done commission quilts for Shamash & Sons Fabrics, Sullivans USA, and Kreinik Thread Manufacturing Company. Linda and her daughter Sarah travel the East Coast of the US, presenting lectures and workshops, and guest teaching at quilt shops. Linda and Sarah also operate "Two Country Quilters," a long-arm machine quilting business. Linda's web page is at: www.twocountryquilters.com

Merry May of Tuckahoe, NJ, began making small quilted items for family and friends in the mid-1970s, not knowing of any quilters in her ancestry at the time. She decided that if she was ever to own a quilt, she would have to make it herself. Since her humble beginnings (which she attributes to "beginner's luck"), Merry has developed a reputation for excellence in teaching quiltmaking, as well as in quilt history, and professional development. She has traveled throughout the East Coast of the US presenting lectures, appraisals and workshops for quilt guilds and quilt shops. Her work is in private and public collections worldwide. Merry is a founding member and currently the President of the State Quilt Guild of NJ, and is also a past president of Tri-State Quiltmaking Teachers (now the Quilt Professionals' Network). In 2002, 2003, 2006 and 2008 she taught at the Vermont Quilt Festival, and for Brother International in 2003. She was nominated by one of her many students for Professional Quilter magazine's 2003 & 2008 Teacher of the Year Award. Merry's web page is at: www.MerryMayhem.com

Linda and Merry also have a new joint venture called "Double Trouble Studios." They are designing quilts using fabrics from the Elizabeth's Studio collection. Check out some of their work at www.DoubleTroubleStudios.com They will also be Quiltin' & Cruisin' to Bermuda in October 2009, and are working on a book entitled, "Insider's Guide to Quilting Careers," whose publication date is targeted for May 2009.

QUESTIONS?
Please call Merry at (609) 628-2256 (Schoolhouse Enterprises) or
Linda at (732) 792-1187
Or, email us:
Linda: Lawnquilt@aol.com · Merry: TwoTonsOfButtons@gmail.com
Merry's web site: www.MerryMayhem.com

Look for Updates on our web site:
www.DoubleTroubleStudios.com

SKILL LEVEL DEFINITIONS

Below you will find some definitions for skill levels as mentioned in our list of workshops. Please note that these are **our** definitions. Other interpretations may vary.

All - just what it sounds like... everyone is welcome, including non-sewers!

Beginner - someone who is familiar with sewing on a sewing machine, but has never done any quilting projects.

Advanced Beginner - someone who is familiar with basic rotary cutting techniques and simple applique.

Intermediate - able to at least complete a wall hanging on their own; is comfortable using rotary cutting techniques, but can also use templates; has had some practice with applique methods; knows how to sew "set-in" seams, curved seams, and mitered corners.

Advanced - is ready for more challenging projects, which may include color and design, drafting original patterns, or being able to tackle a project based on an idea, rather than a specific process. This would be someone who is very experienced in constructing and finishing a variety of quilts.

REGISTRATION

PLEASE COMPLETE THIS FORM AND SEND IT WITH YOUR DEPOSIT (Check or Money Order) Payable to: "Double Trouble Studios" *We accept all major credit cards!*

Name on Card:_____
Signature: _____
Card #:_____
Exp. Date: _____ CVV: _____
Visa ___ MC ___ AmEx ___ Disc ___

Mail to:
Double Trouble Studios
PO Box 305
Tuckahoe, NJ 08250-0305

Saturday, APRIL 25 - Choose ONE Full-Day Class OR ONE Two-Day Class:

_____ Linda Hahn: "Hanafabuki" **Two-Day Class**
___ Merry May: "Machine Quilt as You Go" **One-Day Class**
_____ "Do Your Own Thing" **One-Day**

Sunday, APRIL 26 - Choose ONE Half-Day Class:

_____ Merry May: "3-D Attic Windows"
_____ "Do Your Own Thing"

NAME _____
ADDRESS _____
CITY/STATE/ZIP _____
TELEPHONE #S: DAY: _____ EVENING: _____
CELL: _____
EMAIL: _____
DIETARY RESTRICTIONS (for Saturday Dinner): _____

ROOMMATE'S NAME (if applicable): _____

Every attempt will be made to protect participants and their property, but by signing this contract, I hereby consent to hold harmless any or all of the following: Linda Hahn, Merry May, Double Trouble Studios, The Adventurer Inn, Little Italy Restaurant, Calico 'n Cotton, as well as any or all of their respective employees and assistants.

SIGNATURE REQUIRED: _____
DATE: _____

OFFICE USE ONLY: First Deposit Received: _____ First Deposit Amount: _____ Ck#: _____
Rate: Second Deposit Received: _____ 2nd Deposit Amount: _____ Ck#: _____

Supply Lists Mailed: _____ (Date) Final Confirmation Mailed: _____ (Date)
Other:

ORDER FORM FOR BOOKS & PATTERNS

NAME _____
SHIPPING ADDRESS _____
CITY/STATE/ZIP _____
TELEPHONE #S: DAY: _____ EVENING: _____
CELL: _____
EMAIL: _____

BOOKS & PATTERNS FOR SPRING 2009 BBQ WEEKEND

ITEM	List Price	Our Price	x Quantity	= Amount
"Hanafabuki" Pattern	$ 9.00	$ 8.00	_____	_____
Hobbs Fusible Cotton Batting	$20.00	$17.00	_____	_____

Queen-Size - Will be delivered upon Check-In on Friday Evening

NOTE: One Queen-Size batting will make TWO quilts.

"3-D Attic Windows" Template Set	$19.98	$17.00	_____	_____
		Merchandise Subtotal:		_____
		Priority Mail Shipping:		$ 4.75
		Subtotal:		_____
	7% Sales Tax for NJ Addresses ONLY:			_____
		TOTAL AMOUNT DUE:		_____

Payment Enclosed by: ____ Check *   ____ Money Order   ____ Credit Card:

____ VISA   ____ MasterCard   ____ Discover   ____ American Express

Card #: _____   Expiration Date: _____

Security Code (last 3 digits on signature line on back of card, except AmEx, which is 4 digits on front of card): _____

Name on Credit Card: _____

Signature: _____

Billing Address, if different from Shipping Address, above: _____

_____

* Please make checks payable to: Double Trouble Studios and mail to:

PO Box 305, Tuckahoe, NJ 08250-0305

Bed, Breakfast & Quilt

Fall 2008
Evaluation Form

Thank you for participating in our BBQ Weekend. We'd like your input as to how we can make the weekend more enjoyable for you. Please take a moment and complete the following evaluation and return to us. Please explain your comments on the right side of the evaluation.

CLASSES	Yes, a lot	OK	Not Really	Big NO	COMMENTS HERE
Did you like the class selections offered?	☐	☐	☐	☐	
Did you enjoy the Friday evening activities?	☐	☐	☐	☐	
Do you like that we offer kits for the projects?	☐	☐	☐	☐	
Were the supply lists and pre-cutting easy for you to follow?	☐	☐	☐	☐	
Did the weekend meet your expectations?	☐	☐	☐	☐	
TEACHERS					
Were you able to understand the teacher's instructions?	☐	☐	☐	☐	
Was the teacher easily accessible to you?	☐	☐	☐	☐	
Would you take another class from the BBQ teachers?	☐	☐	☐	☐	
Would you recommend the teachers to your guild?	☐	☐	☐	☐	
ACCOMMODATIONS					
Were the rooms clean and adequate for your needs?	☐	☐	☐	☐	
Were the dinner choices OK?	☐	☐	☐	☐	

ANYTHING ELSE YOU'D LIKE US TO KNOW?

Resources & Contributors

Resources

Please Note: Web sites change frequently! Check our web site at www.DoubleTroubleStudios.com for updates, or to subscribe to our Blog.

Appraisals, Quilt History, Quilt Research:

Alliance for American Quilts - www.centerforthequilt.org/quiltindex.html

American Quilt Study Group - americanquiltstudygroup.org/

American Quilter's Society Appraisal Certification Program - www.americanquilter.com/about_aqs/appraisal_program.php

Quilt History site - www.quilthistory.com

Uniform Standards of Professional Appraisal Practice (USPAP) - www.appraisalfoundation.org/

Blogs:

www.blogger.com
www.blogspot.com
www.typepad.com
www.wordpress.com

Business Issues:

Business Plans:

SCORE - www.score.org

quiltingbusiness.com (charged a $17 fee in 2008)

Microsoft - office.microsoft.com/en-us/templates/TC010175201033.aspx

Credit Card Processing:

PayPal - www.PayPal.com
ProPay - www.ProPay.com

Certifications:

Appraiser:

www.americanquilter.com

Judge:

www.nqaquilts.org

Teacher:

www.nqaquilts.org

Distributors:

Brewer Quilting & Sewing Supplies - www.brewersewing.com

Checker Distributors - www.checkerdist.com

Delaware Dry Goods - www.delawaredg.com

Needlecraft - www.Needlecraftinc.com

Pattern Peddlers - www.thepatternpeddlers.com

Quilter's Dream Batting - www.quiltersdreambatting.com

Quilter's Warehouse - www.quiltersware house.com

QuiltWoman.com - www.QuiltWoman.com

United Notions - www.unitednotions.com

DVD Production:

Casperson, Lars - Angel ThreadsQuilting www.atqsales.com/

Insurance:

Casagrande, Charles - Danskin Agency, Spring Lake, NJ (732) 449-3800 www.danskin-agency.com

Lost Quilt Come Home - www.lostquilt.com/Insuring.html

Lyle, William - www.saqa.com/media/File/insuring_quilts.pdf

The Society of Quilters - chris.johnston@hubinternational.com

Chris Johnston - 1750 E. Glendale Ave. Phoenix, AZ 85020 800-688-7472 ext. 4282

Judging:

Erbach, Lynne - <u>Quilting Quarterly</u> magazine, series of articles on "The Judge's Perspective."

National Quilting Association - www.nqaquilts.com. Look for Judging Certification.

<u>Professional Quilter Magazine</u> - Morna McKeever Golletz, ed. www.professionalquilter.com

Legal Services:

Christina Manuella, Esq., Reed Smith, Princeton, NJ

New Jersey Volunteer Lawyers for the Arts - www.njvla.org

Longarm Quilting Supplies:

Clarke, Pam - Homestitches www.homestitches.com

Columbia River Quilting - 1920 NE 149th Ave., Vancouver, WA 98684 www.columbiariverquilting.com

King's Men Quilting Supply - 2570 N. Walnut St., Rochester, IL 62563 www.kmquiltingsupply.com

Machine Quilter's Business Manager (computer program) - www.eurekadocumentation.com

Quilter's Business Suite (computer program) - www.f2innovations.com

Quilts Complete - www.quiltscomplete.com

Networking:

For All Professional Quilters:

LinkedIn - www.LinkedIn.com This site provides a huge network of professionals who share info and contacts. Merry has established a small but growing group at LinkedIn called the "Professional Quilter's Alliance." Join LinkedIn, set up your Profile, and then type Professional Quilters' Alliance in the "Search

groups" box. This is another example of Merry throwing something out to the universe to see where it lands. Please join us!

Mason-Dixon Quilt Professionals' Network - www.masondixonquiltpros.net (membership required to be listed on web site).

QuiltBiz - Sign up for free at: www.planetpatchwork.com/quiltbiz.htm

Quilt Professionals' Network - www.quiltprofessionalsnetwork.com (membership required to be listed on web site).

QuiltProfessionals Directory - www.quiltprofessionals.com

Yahoo Groups - Go to www.yahoogroups.com and register. Some of the following groups are private lists, and you must be approved by the list moderator before being permitted to participate:
Machine Quilting Professional
Quilt Teach
Quilt Designers

For Guilds:

Heartland Quilt Network - www.heartlandquiltnetwork.com (membership required).

Southern California Council of Quilt Guilds - www.sccqg.org

For Long Arm Quilters:

International Machine Quilters' Association www.imqa.org (membership required to be listed on web site).

For Professional Competitors & Art Quilters:

Studio Art Quilt Associates - www.saqa.com (membership required).

Surface Design Association - www.surfacedesign.org (membership required).

For Quilt Shop Owners:

FabShopNet www.FabShopNet.com (membership required to obtain some benefits, such as their magazine).

Office Supplies:
Office Depot - www.OfficeDepot.com
Quill - www.Quill.com
Reliable - www.reliable.com
Staples - www.Staples.com

Promotional Supplies:
4 Imprint - www.4imprint.com
Amsterdam Printing - www.amsterdam
    printing.com
Modern Postcard - www.modernpostcard.com
Printing for Less - www.printingforless.com
Prints Made Easy - www.printsmadeeasy.com
Vista Printing - www.vistaprint.com

Publishing:
Bar Code:
    GS1 - www.gs1.org/
Books:
    American Quilters' Society - www.
        americanquilter.com. Click on
        "Authors" link, then download
        their *Book Proposal Guidelines*.
    C & T Publishing - www.ctpub.com/
        client/client_pages/Q_submissions.cfm

F+W Media - (formerly Krause)
        www.fwpublications.com/author
        guidelines.asp#crafts
    Leisure Arts - www.leisurearts.com/
    AboutUs/Default.aspx Scroll down to
        "Design Submissions Guide" link to
        down-load their submission info.
    Martingale & Company - www.martin
        gale-pub.com/store/submit_pro
        posal.php
    QuiltWoman.com - www.QuiltWoman.
        com
    Restuccia, Nancy - "Publish Your Pat-
        terns", www.QuiltWoman.com
ISBN:
    RR Bowker - www.isbn.org/standards/
        home/isbn/us/isbnqa.asps
Magazines:

All-American Crafts Publishing – Pub-
    lishers of The Quilter Magazine,
    Fabric Trends. www.thequiltermag.com
American Quilt Retailer - PO Box
    172876, Arlington, TX 76003-2876
    www.americanquiltretailer.com
Better Homes & Gardens -Publishers of
    American Patchwork & Quilting
    Magazine www.allpeoplequilt.com
CK Media, 741 Corporate Circle, Suite
    A, Golden, CO
www.quiltersvillage.com - Publishers of:
    Quilter's Newsletter Magazine,
    Quiltmaker, McCall's Quilting,
    McCall's Quick Quilts, Quilter's
    Home
FabShop News Magazine - PO Box
    820128, Vancouver, WA 98682
    www.fabshopnet.com
Fons & Porter Magazine - www.fons
    andporter.com
Harris Publications - Publishers of
    Quilt Magazine, Quick Quilts,
    Quilt Almanac www.quiltmag.com.
Look for "Contact" link,
then "Editorial Inquiries."
    Professional Quilter - 22412 Rolling
        Hills Lane, Laytonsville, MD
        20882 www.ProfessionalQuilter. com
    Quilting Arts Magazine, www.quilting
        arts.com
    Quilting Now Magazine - 2724 2nd
        Ave., Des Moines, IA 50313
        www.quiltingnow.com
    Quilting Quarterly - c/o NQA, PO
        Box 12190, Columbus, OH
        43212- 0190 www.nqaquilts.org
    Unlimited Possibilities Magazine -
        Meander Publishing, PO Box
        918, Ft. Lupton, CO 80621
        www.upquiltmag.com
Pattern Publishers:
QuiltWoman.com - www.Quilt
    Woman.com

Indygo Junction - PO Box 30238, Kansas City, MO 64112 www.indygojuntioninc.com

McCall's Pattern Company - 615 McCall Road, Manhattan, KS 66502 1-800-255-2762 (Will print tissue paper patterns)

Plastic Bags:
GT Bag - www.GTBag.com
ULine - www.uline.com

Quilt Market - See "Quilt Market" main heading.

Templates:
Carr's Laser Creations, 7910 Sunnybrae Ave, Winnetka, CA 1306SCRCARR@ msn.com

Rulersmith, Inc. – Original producers of the Omnigrid® Ruler. www.rulersmith.com

Quilt Market:
Quilts, Inc. - www.Quilts.com

Quilt Photography:
Web sites containing information on photographing quilts:
Bryer Patch Studio - www.bryerpatch.com
C&T Media Services - www.ctmedia services.com
Hewlett-Packard - www.hp.com
How I Photograph Quilts - www.fun facts.com/photographingquilts
Lost Quilt Come Home - www. lostquilt.com
"Shoot That Quilt!" - www.hollyknott.com

Quilt Shop Owner:
Distributors: See "Distributors" main heading.
Magazines for Shop Owners:
American Quilt Retailer magazine www.americanquiltretailer.com
Professional Quilter magazine www. professionalquilter.com
Networking:
See "Networking" main heading.

Online shop listings:
FabShopHop - www.fabshophop.com/ alumni.asp
QuiltProfessionals - www.quiltprofessionals.com
Quiltropolis - www.quiltropolis.net/ shopsearch.asp
QuiltShops.com - www.quiltshops.com

Office Supplies - see "Office Supplies" main heading.

Quilt Market - See "Quilt Market" main heading.

Shopping Bags:
ULine.com - www.uline.com

Store fixtures:
www.displaywarehouse.com
www.StoreSupply.com

Quilt Show Supplies:
Garden Spot Badge Company (award ribbons) - www.gardenspotribbonaw.com
National Quilting Association (award ribbons) - www.nqaquilts.org

Quilt Shows to Enter:
American Quilter's Society - www.americanquilter.com
Innovations - www.mqinnovations.com
International Quilt Festival - www.quilts.com
Machine Quilters' Exposition - www.mqx show.com
Machine Quilters' Showcase - www.imqa.com
Mancuso Shows - www.quiltfest.com
National Quilting Association - www. nqaquilts.org
NJ Quilt Convention - www.NJQuilts.org
Quilter's Heritage Celebration - www. qhconline.com
Road to California - www.road2ca.com
Vermont Quilt Festival - www.vqf.org

Restoration:
American Quilt Study Group - www. americanquiltstudygroup.org
Daughters of the American Revolution Museum - www.dar.org/museum/

International Quilt Study Center -
Lincoln, NE www.quiltstudy.org
Kirk, Nancy - www.kirkcollection.com
Quilt History site - www.QuiltHistory.com

Shipping:
Bryerpatch Studio - www.bryerpatch.com
Lost Quilt Come Home - www.lostquilt.com
Shipping Supplies:
www.clearbags.com
www.clearenvelopes.com
www.Packagingsupplies.com
ULine, 2105 S. Lakeside Dr., Waukegan,
IL 60085 www.uline.com

Show Management:
Software:
"Quilt Show Manager" by www.eurekadoc
umentation.com

Storage:
Quilt & Textile Storage - www.reddawn.
net/quilt/storage.htm
Lost Quilt Come Home www.lostquilt.com

Teaching:
Certification: NQA Teacher Certification
www.nqaquilts.org
DVD Production:
Angel Threads Quilting http://atqsales.
com/index.php?main_page= contact_us
Networking:
See "Networking" main heading
Online Teaching Opportunities:
www.quiltcampus.net
www.quiltingweekly.com
www.quiltuniversity.com
Other: Professional Quilter magazine
www.professionalquilter.com

Web Site Design:
Web site designers for quilt professionals:
www.gloderworks.com
davidwalker.us.index.html
www.keyweb.com
www.quiltprofessionals.com
www.websitesforquilters.com

Contributors

We sincerely thank those who participated in our research, some of whom participated in more than one area.

Dana Balsamo
Material Pleasures, LLC
Princeton, NJ
732-221-3560
Antique Textile Dealer, Professional Quilt Appraiser
dana@materialpleasures.com
www.materialpleasures.com

Rita B. Barber
Quilters' Heritage Celebration, a production of Barber Diversified,
P.O.Box 503
(18705 Country Club Lane /Shipping Only)
Carlinville, IL 62626,
Phone: 217-854-9323, FAX: 217-854-2209
Quilt Show Manager
rbbarber@qhconline.com
www.qhconline.com

Chuck Casagrande
Danskin Agency
1937 Highway 35
Wall, New Jersey 07719
732-449-3800

Mindy Casperson
Angel Threads Quilting
P.O. Box 500
Mifflinville, PA 18631
570.752.2251
Longarm Quilter, Teacher, Longarm Sales, DVD Production

Kris Driessen
Quiltbug Quilt Shop
169 Main Street
Esperance, NY 12066
888-817-6577
Teacher, Historian, Judge
www.krisdriessen.com

Lorraine Fenstermacher
Pleasant Mount, PA
Longarm Quilter, Friend

Jane M. Hand
Galloway, New Jersey
Quilter, Friend,
Proofreader for Double Trouble Studios

Lacey June Hill
Golden Thyme Designs
P.O.Box 395
Hillsdale, NJ 07642
201-358-2629
Teacher, Pattern Designer
www.laceyjhill.com

Cher Hurney
Former Shop Owner
Qhabitat@aol.com

Doloa Jones
Deloa's Quilt Shop
15804 M-140
South Haven, MI 49090
269.637.4268
Longarm Quilter, Teacher, Longarm Sales

Gail Kessler
Marketing Director
Andover Fabrics
1384 Broadway 15th Fl
New York, NY 10018
212 710 0412
gail@andoverfabrics.com
www.andoverfabrics.com
Ladyfingers Sewing Studio
6375 Oley Turnpike Rd., Oley, PA 19547
ph: 610 689-0068
www.ladyfingerssewing.com

Mark Lipinski
Quilter's Home Magazine
13 Pickle Road
Califon, NJ 07830
Editor, Educator, Designer
www.quiltershomemag.com

Christina M. Manuelli, Esq.
Reed Smith, LLP
P.O. Box 7839
Princeton, New Jersey 08543
   Reed Smith supports and participates in
   New Jersey Volunteer Lawyers for the Arts

Kevin Meszaros, CPA
730 North Broad Street, Suite 100
Woodbury, NJ 08096
856-853-1680
www.meszarosco.com
kmeszaroscpa@aol.com

Miss Rosie's Quilt Co.
Quail Run's Rose Pistola & Carrie Nelson
Rosie ~ Golden Retriever
Best Friend Carrie ~ Quiltmaker, Teacher
... and yes, Rosie comes first
carrie@missrosiesquiltco.com
www.missrosiesquiltco.com

Pat Moore
Former NQA Annual Show Director
www.nqaquilts.org
Carol Newman
Vice President
Quilting-Advertising & Marketing
All American Crafts Publishing, Inc.
newman5@epix.net

Vikki Pignatelli
6620 Forrester Way
Reynoldsburg, OH 43068
614-861-5857
Quilt Artist, Author, Teacher and Lecturer
vikki@vikkipignatelli.com or vikkip@juno.com
www.vikkipignatelli.com

Lyle Sandler
Robin's husband and all around good guy.

Robin L. Sandler
Morganville, NJ 07751

Shop Manager for Creative Sew N Sews
Quilt Finisher for Two Country Quilters
Proof Reader for Double Trouble Studios
Commission Quilter
robinlsandler@hotmail.com

John Scibran
Quilted Bear Den
4068 Albany Post Road
Hyde Park, NY 12538
845-233-4858
Quilt Store Owner, Educator, Long Arm Quilter
info@quiltedbearden.com
www.quiltedbearden.com

Elizabeth Shnayder
Elizabeth's Studio, LLC
732.651.4115
Art Director
www.elizabethsstudio.com
Michele Scott
The Pieceful Quilter
1136 O'Neil St.
Philadelphia, PA 19123
215.627.2484
Quilt Artist, Pattern Designer, Fabric Designer, Educator
michele@piecefulquilter.com
www.piecefulquilter.com

Cyndi Souder
Commission Quilter
www.moonlightinqquilts.com

Lisa Shepard Stewart
Author and Owner, Cultured Expressions
www.CulturedExpressions.com
Marketing Manager, Marcus Fabrics www.MarcusFabrics.com

Rebecca Szabo
1201 Maxim-Southard Rd.
Howell, NJ 07731
732-779-2972
Shop Owner, Commission Quilter, Show Manager
creativesewnsews@aol.com

B.J. Titus
Quilt Artist, Professional Exhibitor
www.bjtitus.com

Geri Wolf
182 Andover Place
Robbinsville, NJ 08691
meadowswoman@aol.com
Teacher, Owner of Threadmakers Getaways
www.threadmakers.com

Jean Ann Wright
5228 Stonevillage Circle
Kennesaw, GA 30152
770-402-5747
Design Consultant to the Quilting Industry, Editor
www.jeanannquilts.com

Madge Ziegler
Bags from Rags
6 Jobs Lane
Newark, DE 19711
Workshops, Lectures, Consultant, Restorations, Commissions, Pattern Designer
Quiltzig@comcast.net

Index

About The Authors

MERRY D. MAY

Merry May of Tuckahoe, NJ, began making quilted pillows for family and friends in the mid-1970s, not knowing at the time that the LeMoyne Star pattern she was making was one of the most difficult patterns to machine piece. She then went on to make her first full-size quilt in the Rolling Star pattern, which is even more difficult than the LeMoyne Star! Since her humble beginnings (which she attributes to "beginner's luck"), Merry has developed a reputation for excellence in teaching quilt making, as well as in collecting and identifying antique quilts. 2008 marks Merry's 20th year of being a quilt instructor.

Merry sometimes refers to herself as a "walking encyclopedia" because of the many requests for information she receives from others in the quilting industry. One of her greatest joys is in passing along information about her experiences in the quilting industry to others; the only "reward" she asks is that those she shares with will in turn "pass it on" to someone else at some point.

In 1992 Merry began writing instructions for "mystery quilts." In 2003 she began using the pen name of "Merry Mayhem's" Mystery Quilts. A mystery quilt's instructions are given out a little at a time so the maker does not know exactly what the quilt will look like until it is nearly finished. Some projects may be completed in a day; others are better when done over a period of months.

Merry is a founding member, past Treasurer, and Past President of the State Quilt Guild of NJ. She is also a past president of Tri-State Quilt making Teachers (now known as the Quilt Professionals' Network), and her local guild, South Shore Stitchers. She is a member of the Down Jersey Folklife Center's Advisory Board.

In 2002, 2003, 2006 and 2008 Merry taught at the Vermont Quilt Festival, and for Brother International in 2003. She was nominated by her students for Professional Quilter magazine's 2003 and 2008 Teacher of the Year. Her work has been published in numerous magazines, exhibited in museums, and is in private collections throughout the US and beyond.

In her "spare" time, she manages a local cemetery. She and her husband, Joe, are the proud owners of two tons of buttons (it seemed like a good idea at the time!).

About The Authors

LINDA J. HAHN

Linda began quilting in 1993 and teaching in 1994. She received her National Quilting Association Teacher Certification in 1999.

Linda has been three times nominated for Professional Quilter Magazine's Teacher of the Year Award (2001, 2004 and 2008) and was also nominated for the NQA Certified Teacher of the Year Award in 2008.

Linda has done commission work for Shamash & Sons Fabric Co., Kreinik Thread Manufacturing, Sullivans, USA and has recently been named Marketing Consultant for Elizabeth's Studio, LLC.

Linda has had work published in The Professional Quilter Magazine, Quilting Now Magazine, Quilt Magazine and Quilt Almanac Magazine.

Linda has taught at the 2005, 2006, 2007 and 2008 New Jersey Quilt Conventions, 2008 National Quilting Association Annual Show, 2009 Quilters Heritage Celebration, 2009 Machine Quilters Exposition, 2009 Mid-Appalachian Quilt Conference. She has also taught in Bermuda twice and on two quilting cruises.

Linda is the 2009 New Jersey All Star at the New Jersey Quilt Convention.

Linda is on the teaching staff at Creative Sew n Sews Quilt Shop in Englishtown, New Jersey.

In addition to teaching, Linda and her daughter, Sarah, own and operate Two Country Quilters, a multi-faceted business out of their home. Two Country Quilters provides long arm quilting services, vends specialty and hard to find quilting items at area quilt shows.

Linda lives in Manalapan, New Jersey with her husband, Allan, daughter, Sarah (an award winning quilter in her own right) and golden retriever, Amber Lynn. When she is not doing something "quilty", (which is rare nowadays) she enjoys cruising the Caribbean, reading trashy novels and watching anything Star Trek or CSI.

DOUBLE TROUBLE STUDIOS
(the partnership)

We've told you about each of us and our individual businesses - now we would like to tell you about our partnership! You may wonder why we choose to include a separate page about our partnership - the book you have just read covers many topics, including mentoring other quilt professionals, working together and different ventures. Together, as partners, we have been able to accomplish even more!

Linda and Merry first met in 1998 at a meeting of The Quilt Professionals Network (which was then known as the Tri-State Quiltmaking Teachers). Together, along with Jeannie Roulet Minchak, they developed and put into action an idea for an annual continuing education conference for quilt professionals (that continues to this day).

After several years acting as co-coordinators of the annual Quilt Professionals Conference, they "passed the baton" on to other members.

Realizing that they worked well together, Linda and Merry decided to try their hands at hosting a quilters' getaway. The "BBQ" (Bed, Breakfast and Quilt) was born! The girls each have their own responsibilities for the different aspects of hosting this activity. BBQs are offered twice a year, in the Spring and in the Fall, and are attended by 30-35 quilters.

In 2006, an opportunity arose for the girls to teach on a quilting cruise. So once again, they worked together, and along with Linda's daughter, Sarah, hosted and guided 67 quilters (including about a dozen husbands) on a quilting cruise to Canada. They will be hosting another quilting cruise in October 2009 to Bermuda.

Opportunity knocked again when the girls were contacted by Elizabeth's Studio, LLC, a new fabric company based in New Jersey, to design and make quilts featuring their fabrics.

It was around this time that they figured it was time to make their partnership "official". After tossing names back and forth, Double Trouble Studios just seemed to fit.

From time to time, Linda and/or Merry would be sought out to answer questions from other quilt professionals. They tossed the idea for this book back and forth - ultimately deciding to "take the plunge" and write it.

Although their personalities and teaching styles are very different, they are complimentary in that they balance each other's strengths and weaknesses.

Linda credits Merry for mentoring and guiding her through her quilt professional journey. Merry credits Linda with having the drive to get things done and following through on long-term, complicated projects.